Assessment of Learning Assistance Services

C. Walvekar, *Editor*

)IRECTIONS FOR COLLEGE LEARNING ASSISTANCE
.V. LAURIDSEN, *Editor-in-Chief*

5, September 1981

.p   .k sourcebooks in
`h(ey-Bass Higher Education Series

WITHDRAWN

Jossey-Bass Inc., Publishers
San Francisco • Washington • London

Assessment of Learning Assistance Services
Number 5, 1981, September 1981
Carol C. Walvekar, *Editor*

New Directions for College Learning Assistance Series
Kurt V. Lauridsen, *Editor-in-Chief*

New Directions for College Learning Assistance is published quarterly
by Jossey-Bass Inc., Publishers. Subscriptions, single-issue orders,
change of address notices, undelivered copies, and other
correspondence should be sent to *New Directions* Subscriptions,
Jossey-Bass Inc., Publishers, 433 California Street, San Francisco,
California 94104.

Editorial correspondence should be sent to the Editor-in-Chief,
Kurt V. Lauridsen, Director, Student Learning Center,
University of California, Berkeley, California 94720.

Library of Congress Catalogue Card Number LC 81-48471

International Standard Serial Number ISSN 0271-0617

International Standard Book Number ISBN 87589-808-4

Cover art by Willi Baum
Manufactured in the United States of America

Ordering Information

The paperback sourcebooks listed below are published quarterly and can be ordered either by subscription or as single copies.

Subscriptions cost $35.00 per year for institutions, agencies, and libraries. Individuals can subscribe at the special rate of $21.00 per year *if payment is by personal check.* (Note that the full rate of $35.00 applies if payment is by institutional check, even if the subscription is designated for an individual.) Standing orders are accepted.

Single copies are available at $7.95 when payment accompanies order, and *all single-copy orders under $25.00 must include payment.* (California, Washington, D.C., New Jersey, and New York residents please include appropriate sales tax.) For billed orders, cost per copy is $7.95 plus postage and handling. (Prices subject to change without notice.)

To ensure correct and prompt delivery, all orders must give either the *name of an individual* or an *official purchase order number.* Please submit your order as follows:

Subscriptions: specify series and subscription year.
Single Copies: specify sourcebook code and issue number (such as, CLA8).

Mail orders for United States and Possessions, Latin America, Canada, Japan, Australia, and New Zealand to:
Jossey-Bass Inc., Publishers
433 California Street
San Francisco, California 94104

Mail orders for all other parts of the world to:
Jossey-Bass Limited
28 Banner Street
London EC1Y 8QE

New Directions for College Learning Assistance Series
Kurt V. Lauridsen, *Editor-in-Chief*

Contents

Editor's Notes

In spite of the proliferation of books, articles, and studies on educational evaluation, the topic of learning assistance evaluation has not been extensively discussed. The purpose of this volume is to give greater definition and direction to the field of learning assistance evaluation.

Boylan, in the first chapter of this sourcebook, maintains that evaluation of learning assistance is in an infant stage of development. He identifies the issues, needs, and realities that face our profession as we try to establish identities and to evaluate our way into the world of academe. Boylan recommends that we develop models of evaluation that can be generalized to the diversity of existing programs.

In his chapter on methodology, Clowes constructs a type of model requested by Boylan. Clowes's model pulls together not only the evaluation of developmental, remedial, and learning assistance programs, but also the utilization of qualitative and quantitative methodologies to evaluate those three types of programs.

Because learning assistance programs represent a diversity of people, institutions, and politics, speaking generally about evaluation practice is not an easy task. Moore, however, proves equal to the task in his chapter on role and scope. He categorizes evaluation design into frameworks, demonstrates their applicability to the field of learning assistance, focuses on one model that is especially suitable, and ties it into local purposes and practices of evaluation.

The need to evaluate in order to demonstrate our contribution to the institutions we serve has been ever-present for administrators of learning assistance. However, the demonstration of our worth in terms of research studies has been unconvincing to say the least. In their first chapter, Majer and Myers offer simple yet detailed advice in setting up experimental and quasi-experimental research designs to answer four types of research questions. They also discuss the results of four studies in which these designs were applied. In their second chapter, Myers and Majer offer many practical suggestions for using computers for data collection.

Walvekar's chapter on evaluation of learning describes a process for assessing abilities, interests, and achievements of learning from entry to exit in a learning assistance program. This chapter identifies problems in using tests to measure learning and suggests ways to use them in spite of their shortcomings.

In their chapter, Smith and Brown elaborate on the value of staff performance appraisal and discuss its contribution to staff development.

1

Both theoretical and practical ideas are stressed in this volume. The authors confront philosophical differences between developmental, remedial, and learning assistance terminology; present and apply evaluation models; outline and apply research designs; detail recommendations for setting up computer-based collection systems; and offer practical suggestions for staff performance and learning evaluation. Finally, they attempt to move evaluation of learning assistance programs out of its crib and into the world.

Carol Clymer Walvekar
Editor

*Carol Clymer Walvekar is the assistant director of study skills
and tutorial services at the University of Texas at El Paso.
She worked as the coordinator of services at the Center for
Learning Assistance at New Mexico State University for five
years and received her Ed.D. from New Mexico State in 1978.
Walvekar edits a column on evaluation for the* Western
College Reading Association Newsletter *and has consulted
for learning assistance programs on a national basis.*

*Learning assistance program evaluation has become
increasingly important in the past decade, yet the
level of typical program evaluation practices remains
relatively unsophisticated. Learning center
professionals must confront the major evaluation
issues in the field in order to improve the current
level of practice.*

Program Evaluation:
Issues, Needs, and Realities

Hunter R. Boylan

It is said that Frederick Barbarossa of Prussia once attempted to evaluate whether or not man possessed a soul by weighing a peasant before and after having him killed. Working on the assumption that the soul left the body when a person died, Frederick compared the unfortunate peasant's weight before and after death to determine if there were any significant differences. Since Frederick's measures indicated no weight loss between pretest and posttest, he concluded that man did not possess a soul. When one of his courtiers suggested that perhaps it was only this particular peasant who lacked a soul, Frederick reportedly admitted to some limitations in the validity of his study.

Fortunately, measurement and evaualation have advanced considerably since such early efforts. A governing body of theoretical constructs has been developed, a voluminous literature exists, a variety of methodologies have been identified, and a set of standards and ethics now governs the application of evaluation. Presumably, these advances should discourage present-day uses of Barbarossa's methodology.

Unfortunately, this is not always the case. More often than not, the evaluation activities of learning assistance programs are only slightly more sophisticated than those of Frederick Barbarossa. After all, Frederick was able to identify the topic he wished to study, devise a measure, administer a

C. C. Walvekar (Ed.), *New Directions for College Learning Assistance: Assessment of Learning Assistance Services*, no. 5. San Francisco: Jossey-Bass, 1981.

pretest and a posttest, analyze the results, and report his findings. But, he also failed to define the problem adequately, selected inappropriate measures, neglected to control for confounding variables, and generalized on the basis of insufficient data.

Those familiar with the state of the art as applied to many learning assistance programs will recognize some of the "Barbarossa methodology" in current efforts. As Grant and Hoeber (1978, p. 31) point out, "Many programs have been hastily and poorly designed, lack clear goals and objectives, and have inadequate procedures for data collection." As a consequence, such evaluation activities, like Frederick's, may contribute to the demise of the subject and still fail to generate useful information.

While the quality of evaluation efforts typically undertaken in learning assistance programs is poor, it may not be completely fair to fault the programs or their staff for this shortcoming. Any evaluation involving human performance is far more complicated than the evaluation of inanimate objects. Also, evaluation in postsecondary education is a relatively recent phenomenon. Most educational programs were not held accountable for evaluating outcomes until two decades ago. As a result, the practice of educational evaluation in postsecondary settings is still in relative infancy. Few generally agreed-upon methodologies for assessing learning outcomes have been developed, and those that have are subject to many limitations.

Perhaps most important, the field of learning assistance is also fairly new. Devirian, Enright, and Smith (1975); Cross (1976); and Roueche and Snow (1977) have all pointed out that most programs designed to serve underprepared college learners were implemented after the late 1960s. Because the field is still in an early stage of development, many critical issues relating to evaluation remain unresolved. Primary among those issues are questions relating to the definition, role, and scope of learning assistance activities. Before discussing procedural issues in learning assistance evaluation, therefore, it may be appropriate to define the broader context in which learning assistance activities take place.

A Context for Program Evaluation

Terms such as *developmental education, basic studies,* or *learning assistance* are frequently misunderstood and misused. They are often used interchangeably to describe activities designed to improve student learning. In the author's view, however, they are not interchangeable. Each term refers to a specific concept or activity, and the failure to distinguish between them contributes to confusion in the field. The situation might be compared to an automobile designer who is unable to discriminate between the functions of engines, transmissions, and wheels. His resulting automotive product might, with luck, be roadworthy. It is more likely that a lot of motion would take place among component parts, but the vehicle would not run at all. And attempts to improve the design would be limited to rearrangement of components that might work only by chance. If learning assistance program personnel are to evaluate and improve their activities, they should understand some of the basic design issues that underlie learning assistance programs.

In looking at definitions and program design, it might be fair to view developmental education as a general class of activities under which all other terms are subsumed. Developmental education is a holistic term that refers to a field of study, a field of research, and a field of practice. It focuses on a specific clientele—college students.

Viewed in this manner, developmental education is much like any other subdiscipline in education, such as early childhood, special education, or educational psychology. Researchers investigate major issues in the field and report their findings in the literature; instructors train practitioners on the basis of this research and literature; and practitioners provide services based upon what they have learned about the field. All of these individuals, however, are involved in the general field of developmental education.

All of them also make certain assumptions about students that form their philosophies and guide their practices. They assume, for instance, that practically all adults are capable of mastering basic academic skills and developing their existing skills in other areas. They further assume that academic excellence is a worthwhile goal and that, given proper instruction and support, practically all students have the capacity for meeting fairly high academic standards. They also assume that the best way to promote skill development is to accept each student's individual level of development and to build upon it. Finally, they make an overriding assumption that all adults have a right to the benefits of higher education, and that it is possible and desirable to promote individual skill development as part of an "open door" policy in higher education. These assumptions are generally considered to comprise the philosophy of developmental education, regardless of the setting in which it takes place.

The programs based upon the developmental education philosophy are identified by various titles such as developmental education programs, basic studies programs, learning assistance centers, study skills centers, academic improvement programs, and so forth. In practice, a difference in titles does not necessarily reflect a difference in structure, services, or mission. In theory, however, specific types of programs can be identified: remedial/preparatory programs, basic studies programs, and learning assistance programs.

In defining remedial/preparatory programs, K. Patricia Cross (1976, p. 31) suggests that they are designed "to overcome academic deficiencies . . . in the standard dictionary sense in which remediation is concerned with correcting weaknesses." Programs offering services exclusively for the purpose of preparing students for introductory college-level work—particularly if participation in such programs is a condition for college entry—are remedial/preparatory in nature. These programs may include classroom instruction, learning laboratory activity, support services such as counseling or diagnosis, or combinations of all three.

Basic studies programs are curriculum-oriented and serve more than simply remedial functions. The program may provide academic support services such as advising and tutoring but its primary purpose is to provide instruction, usually in a fixed curriculum and in a classroom setting. Participation in a basic studies program is not usually required as a condition of admission. Basic studies programs frequently provide a broad range of classroom instruction, which may include some remedial courses but is usually aimed at developing existing skills. As a result, most basic studies courses are offered for some sort of college credit.

Learning assistance programs differ from basic studies programs in that they usually do not offer classroom instruction. The emphasis is, instead, on providing a variety of services designed to facilitate learning. These services frequently include diagnosis and placement, counseling, tutoring, reading and study skills development, and individualized learning activities. Like the basic studies programs, learning assistance programs also serve students at a variety of levels. Ideally, such programs also go "beyond just basic skills to help in all academic subjects and even to assisting a student or faculty member with personal problems" (Christ, 1979, p. 8).

Often all three types of programs may be found on the same campus. Where all three types of programs exist simultaneously, fairly clear distinctions are made between the role, scope, and function of each. Where only one of the three types of programs exists, that program will frequently include some of the services or functions of the other programs. This situation probably contributes to the confusion in definition of program mission, role, and scope. The confusion, in turn, contributes to the difficulty associated with evaluation of learning assistance programs.

The comments made in this chapter will refer specifically to learning assistance activities involving a broad range of services provided outside the classroom for students at all levels as well as faculty and staff. Nevertheless, many of these comments may be equally applicable to other types of developmental education delivery systems.

Evaluation Measurement Issues

Previous efforts in evaluating learning assistance programs have focused on the following measures:

- Student grade point averages
- Gain scores from pretest to posttest on standardized or locally developed achievement measures
- Ratings of student satisfaction with program services
- Student retention

One or more of these measures has been applied to practically all service components of learning assistance programs. Donovan (1975), for instance, reported that students who received at least four hours per week of tutoring in basic courses earned mean grade point averages of 2.33 while those who did not averaged only 2.00. Similar results were reported by Slawsky (1978), who found that those students utilizing tutorial services earned a higher percentage of A's and B's than those who did not.

Brown (1974) also used student grade point averages to assess the effectiveness of peer-counseling activities, such as those frequently provided through learning assistance programs. His results indicated that students who were exposed to a systematic peer-counseling program earned higher grade point averages than those who were not.

A number of studies also used grade point average to evaluate the impact of college reading programs. Fairbanks (1974) found that programs that included diagnosis, counseling, and individualization and required consistent commitment of student time—all of which seem to characterize learning assistance program efforts—tended to result in higher student grade point averages. Those findings were supported by the studies of Turner and others (1974), Burgess and others (1976), and Haburton (1977).

Gain scores on standardized and locally developed instruments have also been used to evaluate learning assistance services. Kulik and others (1974) reviewed the literature on individualized instruction supported by tutoring and self-paced materials and found that practically all studies showed substantial gains from pretest to posttest on a variety of achievement measures. These results were supported by Cross (1976) in her review of individualized instruction. Both authors, however, cited methodology weaknesses in the studies reviewed.

In other areas, Donovan (1975) reported raw score gains of approximately 30 points on the Nelson-Denny reading test for students participating in a reading and tutorial laboratory in a community college. Boylan and Whimbey (1978) reported gain scores of up to 100 percent on a criterion-referenced mathematics test for students participating in a mathematics assistance laboratory. Brown (1974) demonstrated that peer counseling services were correlated with significant student gains on the Brown-Holtzman Survey of Study Habits and Attitudes.

Students' expressed level of satisfaction with program services is a frequently used evaluation measure in learning assistance programs. Program reports by Broadbent (1977), Kennebrew (1975), and Rachavong (1979) all cite student satisfaction as an indication of the program's success in meeting student needs. The most typically used measures of student satisfaction involve some sort of a rating scale for program services as well as space for open-ended comments. In general, it appears that students who use learning assistance program services tend to rate these services highly—particularly those students who use the services on a regular basis.

Maxwell (1979, p. 188) suggests that rating forms should also be combined with less obtrusive measures of student satisfaction such as the number of their friends that students have referred to the learning assistance program. Faculty ratings of learning assistance program services based on their experiences with students who have been referred to the program also provide useful evaluative feedback.

Student retention has also been used to assess the effectiveness of learning assistance program services. Donovan (1975) cites a rate of retention in school through the senior year that is approximately 15.5 percent greater for participants in a learning assistance program than for nonparticipants as evidence of that program's success. In a regional survey of learning assistance programs, LePage and Zachel (1978) found that the average year-to-year retention rate for participants was about 66 percent. While the authors did not determine what the rate of retention was for nonparticipants, other studies (Ludwig and Gold, 1969; Snyder and Blocker, 1970) suggest that year-to-year retention rates for underprepared students who do not receive assistance range from 30 to 55 percent.

In addition to these measures, several other means of assessing learning assistance programs have been suggested. Maxwell (1979) suggested that repeated voluntary utilization of learning assistance services by students is a valid indicator of the effectiveness of those services. She also suggests that faculty and staff attitudes toward the program, as evidenced by their involvement with it and the number of students they refer to the program, may be used as measures of the program's success.

Spivey (1981) recommends the use of goal attainment scaling, developed by Kiresuk and Sherman (1968), to measure the effectiveness of learning assistance services. In this system, students and staff agree upon specific objectives for skills development, determine weighting scales for each area of development, agree upon achievement measures, and evaluate progress toward attaining goals at the end of a specified period of time. A rating formula is then applied to evaluate the degree of progress made by each student. This is a fairly sophisticated measurement technique and one that requires a degree of training in order to implement. It is, however, a highly useful form of measurement that can provide valuable information about individual student progress, as well as information on program impact.

All of these measures have been applied at one time or another, using various design formats to assess the impact of learning assistance programs and services. Unfortunately, all of them also have certain limitations that can compromise the validity of evaluation activities.

Limitations of Typical Evaluation Measures

Grade Point Averages. The use of grade point averages as a measurement device has often been questioned. It is difficult, for instance, to assess the impact of any specific activity on grade point averages. To develop a comprehensive picture of each service's contribution to student achievement, Suen (1979) arrived at a formula using stepwise regression to weigh the impact of various services on student grade point averages. However, this technique requires rather sophisticated statistical skills and still does not account for other variables that may have an impact upon student grade point average. Such items as the difficulty of students' courses during a given academic term, intervening personal problems, or individual differences in student motivation may all contribute positively or negatively to student achievement. It is practically impossible to isolate all the factors that may affect grade point average independently of whatever services are provided. Overall grade point average, therefore, is useful only as a very generalized measure of total program performance. Even then, this measure is confounded by a number of variables that are difficult to identify and even more difficult to control.

Individual grades in particular courses may be more useful as measures of specific services. Grades in courses for which a student is being tutored, for instance, may provide some indication of the effectiveness of specific tutoring activities. Variables other than tutoring, however, may still affect a student's performance in a given course and thus constitute a limit to the validity of grades as a measurement device.

Gain Scores. Gain scores from pretest to posttest are subject to limitations brought about by the so-called interactive effect of pretesting. Exposure to items on a pretest may serve to condition responses on the posttest, leading to improved performance that is not related to the treatment. Another limitation has to do with the fact that gain scores are not necessarily correlated with behavior. Students may, for instance, show marked gains on a paper and pencil test of reading skills and still not read more books or study more effectively.

The use of commercial, norm-referenced tests to assess student gain may also limit the validity of gain scores as a measure of program service impact. These tests are usually designed to discriminate between students of differing ability levels. The questions on norm-referenced tests are selected because they produce variability in scores.

In contrast, gain score assessment is not designed to produce variability but to determine how much a student may have learned with regard to specific learning tasks. Consequently, many of the commercial norm-referenced tests available may be inappropriate as measures of how far a student has actually progressed. To control for this, it is necessary either to screen available norm-referenced tests to make sure that the questions are consistent with the specific learning tasks one wishes to measure or to generate criterion-referenced tests based upon desired levels of proficiency on specific tasks. (Popham [1971] provides a more detailed discussion of criterion-referenced versus norm-referenced measurement.)

Student Satisfaction. Student satisfaction measures are often limited by various forms of bias. First of all, questions are often constructed in such a way as to produce favorable responses. Also, the settings in which rating forms are administered or the behaviors of those administering the rating forms may bias the results. Research on student evaluations of faculty (Centra, 1979) suggests that student ratings can be influenced by a variety of instructor behaviors that have little relationship to actual learning. Even if students report their levels of satisfaction with accuracy, their satisfaction with a given learning experience may be influenced by prior attitudes toward learning or experiences unrelated to program services.

Student satisfaction ratings often do not control for variability in student usage of program services. The level of satisfaction of a student who has attended only two study skills sessions, for instance, may be given the same weight as that of a student who has attended twenty sessions. If student satisfaction ratings are to accurately reflect the quality of program services, the ratings should be able to differentiate between those students who have used the services frequently and those who have not.

Finally, the relationship between student satisfaction ratings and actual skills development has yet to be established. Such ratings are limited because they apply only to the quality of experience with a given service and not to the quality of learning that may have taken place.

Student Retention. Retention rates are an even more generalized measure of program impact than grade point averages. As with grade point averages, it is probably impossible to isolate all of the factors that may contribute to student retention. Even if those factors could be isolated, it would still be extremely difficult to control for their effects.

Also, retention figures may not accurately represent the quality of program services. If, as a result of his participation in career counseling services, a university student decides that his career interests can best be served by leaving the university and enrolling in a community college, then the program has, in fact, provided a valuable service to the student. Nevertheless, this student's attrition would be counted negatively in assessing the learning assistance program.

Similarly, some students may drop out of the institution for a brief period because of a transient problem, and then return later. It is difficult to track these students or to know how to count them in retention figures.

Such difficulties in interpreting the meaning of retention rates limit their application as measures of program performance.

Nevertheless, there seems to be a fairly consistent positive correlation between effective learning assistance services and retention among participants. As Astin (1975, p. 148) has pointed out, "anything that can be done to enhance students' academic performance will also tend to reduce attrition rates." Consequently, student retention may be a useful, if generalized, measure of program performance.

The limitations of many learning assistance program evaluation measures tend to make program evaluation difficult. To a degree, these limitations may be controlled through careful evaluation design. Given the vagueness of human performance measures, however, some limitations will always exist. This situation should not prevent learning assistance program personnel from assessing the outcomes of their activities using the best methods and measures currently available. In fact, it is likely that as more evaluation activity takes place in learning assistance programs, more information will be available to improve the quality of these evaluation activities. This information must then be shared with other professionals in the field in order to address some of the major evaluation needs confronting learning assistance programs.

Current Needs in Evaluation

If necessity is, indeed, the mother of invention, then the activities of learning assistance programs should generate inventive responses to some major evaluation needs in the coming years. The extent to which these inventive responses are forthcoming may have considerable bearing on the long-range impact of learning assistance programs in postsecondary education. At least four such needs are immediate: (1) learning assistance program component assessment; (2) standardized evaluation models; (3) improved data collection, storage, and retrieval; and (4) improved reporting of evaluation models and outcomes.

Component Assessment. With a few notable exceptions, learning assistance programs have developed by accretion. That is, they have usually grown by adding services and staff in a near-random manner. As money has become available, new services or additional staff have been included in programs. As problems are identified, new services or alternative delivery systems are implemented. Unfortunately, this growth has been largely unimpeded by planning and unencumbered by research. As funding becomes static or declines, this process will no longer suffice. It will then be necessary to carefully plan either the addition or the deletion of program services.

In order for this to be accomplished in the most cost-effective manner, program managers will need to know which services or combinations of services yield the best return in terms of student performance. They will also need to know which delivery systems are most effective for providing these services. This will require additional research on the individual components of learning assistance programs and their relationship to each other. It will be necessary to know the most effective means of assessing student aptitudes and learning styles. Given these various aptitudes and styles, it will also be necessary to identify the best possible ways of accommodating them through learning assistance services. The services themselves should be assessed to determine their strengths, applications, and limitations. Does tutoring, for instance, work best when combined with counseling or individualized learning activity, or both? Do reading and study skills activities have a greater impact on student performance than subject-specific tutoring? Do individualized learning activities have equal applicability to all basic skills areas, or are some areas better addressed through other strategies? The answers to these and other questions must be found through program evaluation and research if learning assistance programs are to accomplish their goals in a more efficient and cost-effective manner.

Standardized Evaluation Models. At present, individual learning assistance programs evaluate their activities using a wide range of methods and measures. There is little consistency in evaluation designs or measures. Where gain scores are used, for instance, different instruments are used to assess gain. Even when the same instruments are used in different programs, one program may report results in raw scores, another in percentiles, and still another in grade level equivalents. As a result, it is very difficult to establish consistent performance criteria for learning assistance programs. Even where program evaluation results are available, there is no way of comparing one program with another if the evaluation data are not reported in a consistent fashion.

This heterogeneity in evaluation methods and measures may be appropriate right now. As different approaches are tested in practice, those which are the most useful, valid, and manageable, will become apparent. They might then serve as models for other evaluation activities.

At some point, however, there will need to be a consensus in the field regarding the best methods of evaluating learning assistance programs and reporting the outcomes of evaluation activities. When this consensus is reached and standardized models are developed, evaluation will become more simplified, and research on services and delivery systems will be easier to conduct. This, in turn, will lead to a greater understanding of how learning assistance programs can best function to serve the needs of their students. It will also provide a valuable reference point for programs that may just be initiating evaluation projects or that intend to upgrade the quality of their evaluation efforts.

Data Collection, Storage, and Retrieval. Evaluation of programs requires the collection, storage, and retrieval of vast quantities of information. In order to facilitate evaluation, systems for collecting, storing, and retrieving information must be developed. Such systems are the cornerstone of any systematic evaluation effort. As yet, however, few models for managing information required for learning assistance evaluation are available.

Learning assistance programs often collect data on a random basis, store it in different locations, and then have difficulty retrieving it for evaluation purposes. Even when records are consistently maintained and adequate storage and retrieval capacities exist, most of the program record keeping is done manually. Commitment of time and resources to this laborious, time-consuming process is frequently difficult to justify.

Two needs are, therefore, apparent. One is for generalizable models of program information-gathering systems. The other is for simplified methods of storing and retrieving information. The response to the first need will undoubtedly come from sharing among practitioners through the literature, through conferences, and through other professional development activities. The second need is likely to be accommodated through improved application of institutional computers and microprocessors. In order to avail themselves of relatively low-cost technology to facilitate information management, learning assistance program personnel will need to enhance their knowledge of this new technology.

Reporting of Models and Outcomes. Learning assistance is somewhat unique in that much of the new knowledge in the field is generated by practitioners rather than by researchers. Unfortunately, most practitioners do not have the time or the inclination to write books, monographs, or articles reporting the results of their activities. Nevertheless, a great need exists for practitioners to share their knowledge with each other and to identify the best models available through this sharing process. This is particularly true insofar as program evaluation models are concerned.

This volume of the *New Directions for College Learning Assistance* series is one attempt to meet this need. Publications such as the *Journal of Developmental and Remedial Education* and the Western College Reading Association's new *WCRA Journal* offer other avenues for practitioners to report the results of their evaluation activities. The ERIC system represents still another method of disseminating information from program reports and evaluations. All of these vehicles must be used more consistently by practitioners.

More informal networks for sharing evaluation information are also necessary. Professional association newsletters such as those of the National Association of Remedial/Developmental Studies, the Western College Reading Association, or the American College Personnel Association's Commission XVI might serve in this capacity. In addition, regional

14

and national conferences of these professional associations should serve as forums for discussion of evaluation issues and models.

As evaluation activities and models are described, reported, and discussed through a variety of information-sharing networks, it is likely that consensus on major issues will emerge and appropriate models for evaluation activities will be developed. It is vitally important, however, that information about program evaluation be included in the professional communication network and that the network be expanded if new models are to be developed and disseminated.

Conclusion

According to *Webster's New Collegiate Dictionary*, the word *evaluate* is a verb meaning "to determine or fix the value of." The professionals involved in learning assistance programs obviously believe that their activities are of value to their institutions, their students, and, in the long run, their society. Unfortunately, since they are the "new kids" on the educational block, they are constantly asked to prove the value of their services. A lament frequently heard at developmental education conferences is that "Nobody asks the History Department to justify their existence, and yet their budget is three times larger than the learning assistance program's." Like many new or innovative activities, learning assistance programs operate in environments where the traditional is often valued regardless of its productivity or cost-effectiveness. As a result, learning assistance programs are challenged to prove their worth or to justify why resources should be committed to their activities when the resources could be used for faculty salaries or research. The fairness of this situation may be debatable. The reality of it is not.

Perhaps it is time for those involved with learning assistance programs to accept the reality of their environment and to respond aggressively to the challenge it presents. The interests of learning assistance programs will not be served by refusing to "determine or fix the value of" their services. They will be served by assessing what learning assistance programs do, determining how well it is done, and describing the benefits that result from having done it. If learning assistance is to have any relevance at all, its value must be determined, measured, and reported.

Evaluation, therefore, should not be viewed as an unpleasant chore done simply to please unappreciative colleagues or administrators. Instead, it should be looked upon as an opportunity to understand better what is being done, to improve it, and to establish its value.

References

Astin, A. W., *Preventing Students from Dropping Out*. San Francisco: Jossey-Bass, 1975.

Boylan, H. R., and Whimbey, A. "Cognitive Skills-Oriented PSI: A 'Second Generation' Model of the Keller Plan." Paper presented at fifth National Conference on Personalized Instruction, Washington, D.C., May 1978.

Broadbent, W. "Leeward Community College: Developmental Education Study." Honolulu, Hawaii: Leeward Community College Developmental Education Program, 1977.

Brown, W. F. "Effectiveness of Paraprofessionals: The Evidence." *Personnel and Guidance Journal,* 1974, *53* (4), 257-263.

Burgess, B. A., and others. "Effect on Academic Achievement of a Voluntary Reading Program." *Journal of Reading,* 1976, *19,* 644-646.

Centra, J. A. *Determining Faculty Effectiveness.* San Francisco: Jossey-Bass, 1979.

Christ, F. L. "An Interview with Frank Christ," by Nancy Spann. *Journal of Developmental and Remedial Education,* 1979, *3* (1), 8-11.

Cross, K. P. *Accent on Learning: Improving Instruction and Reshaping the Curriculum.* San Francisco: Jossey-Bass, 1976.

Devirian, M. C., Enright, G., and Smith, G. D. "A Survey of Learning Center Programs in U.S. Institutions of Higher Education." *Proceedings of the Eighth Annual Conference of the Western College Reading Association,* 1975, *8,* 69-76.

Donovan, R. A. *National Project II: Alternatives to the Revolving Door.* New York: Bronx Community College, 1975.

Fairbanks, M. M. "The Effect of College Reading Programs on Academic Achievement." In P. L. Nache (Ed.), *Interaction: Research and Practice for College-Adult Reading.* Twenty-third yearbook. Clemson, S.C.: National Reading Conference, 1974.

Grant, M. K., and Hoeber, D. R. *Basic Skills Programs: Are They Working?* Higher Education Research Report No. 1. Washington, D.C.: AAHE-ERIC, 1978.

Haburton, E. "Impact of an Experimental Reading-Study Skills Course on High-Risk Student Success in a Community College." In P. D. Pearson and J. Hansen (Eds.), *Reading: Theory, Research and Practice.* Twenty-sixth yearbook. Clemson, S.C.: National Reading Conference, 1977.

Kinnebrew, E. L. "Project 30: An Evaluation and Review." Sacramento, CA: Project 30 Report, Sacramento City College, 1975.

Kiresuk, T. J., and Sherman, R. E. "Goal Attainment Scaling: A General Method for Evaluating Comprehensive Mental Health Programs." *Community Mental Health Journal,* 1968, *4,* 443-453.

Kulik, J. A., Kulik, C. L., and Carmichael, K. "The Keller Plan in Science Teaching." *Science,* 1974, *183,* 379-383.

LePage, H. L., and Zachel, G. O. "Survey of Middle-Size Institutions in Selected Midwestern States." *Learning Centers in Higher Education.* Report No. 1. La Crosse, Wis.: American College Personnel Association Commission XVI, 1978.

Ludwig, L., and Gold, B. K. "The Developmental Studies and Tutorial Programs: A Progress Report." Los Angeles: Los Angeles City College, 1969.

Maxwell, M. *Improving Student Learning Skills: A Comprehensive Guide to Successful Practices and Programs for Increasing Performance of Underprepared Students.* San Francisco: Jossey-Bass, 1979.

Popham, J. W. (Ed.). *Criterion-Referenced Measurement: An Introduction.* Englewood Cliffs, N.J.: Educational Technology Publications, 1971.

Rachavong, D. "A Report of the Freshman Basic Studies Program." Charleston: West Virginia State College, 1979.

Roueche, J. E., and Snow, J. J. *Overcoming Learning Problems: A Guide to Developmental Education in College.* San Francisco: Jossey-Bass, 1977.

Slawsky, M., and Slawsky, Z. "First Aid for Physics." *Change,* 1978, *10* (1), 59.

Snyder, F., and Blocker, C. E. "Persistence of Developmental Students." Harrisburg, Pa.: Harrisburg Area Community College, 1970.

Spivey, N. "Goal Attainment in the College Learning Center." *Journal of Developmental and Remedial Education*, 1981, *4* (2), 11–13.

Suen, H. "Special Services Evaluation." *Journal of Developmental and Remedial Education*, 1979, *3* (1), 7.

Turner, C. S., and others. "The Effects of a Developmental Program on University Grades." *Journal of Reading*, 1974, *17*, 531–537.

Hunter R. Boylan is the director of the Kellogg Institute
for the Training and Certification of Developmental
Educators and a professor in Appalachian State University's
graduate program in developmental education. He
is currently serving as president of the National
Association for Remedial/Developmental Studies
in Postsecondary Education.

Classifying types of learning assistance programs and evaluation methods can guide in selecting the appropriate method of evaluation.

Evaluation Methodologies for Learning Assistance Programs

Darrel A. Clowes

Is there one best way to evaluate learning assistance programs? I think not. The idea of one best way for anything implies that we know what anything is and that anything is one thing. I do not think this claim can be made either for learning assistance programs or for evaluation. Both learning assistance programs and evaluation must be seen as multidimensional concepts. This chapter proposes a manageable way to classify types of learning assistance programs and types of evaluation so that appropriate methods of evaluation can be selected for particular learning assistance programs.

Learning Assistance Programs

What is a learning assistance program? Christ (1971) has provided two definitions, but they do not give me a sense of a single clear entity. On the same page, he defines a learning assistance program as "a facility where students (learners) come to effect change in their learning assistance skills and attitudes" and as "any place where learners, learning data, and learning facilitators are interwoven in a sequential, cybernetic, individual-

C. C. Walvekar (Ed.), *New Directions for College Learning Assistance: Assessment of Learning Assistance Services*, no. 5. San Francisco: Jossey-Bass, 1981.

ized, people-oriented system to service all students (learners) and faculty (learning facilitators) of any institution for whom learning by its students is important" (1971, p. 35). The two definitions appear unrelated. The first stresses the notion of purposeful change on the part of students in their attitudes and learning skills. The second definition does not accommodate the idea of purposeful change but portrays the learning assistance program (LAP) as a system within which learning occurs. In this definition, it is difficult to distinguish the LAP from a library, a computer center, or even a firing range on a military training base. What then is a LAP? And why do I belabor the point?

LeRoy Sullivan (1979) recently completed a survey of learning centers in higher education. In 673 pages, he has codified and recodified his data on learning centers; in the United States alone, he identified 1,778 distinct learning center programs. However, nowhere is there a single definition of a LAP. The report of the survey's findings states "Conceptually, these learning centers represent an amalgamation in various combinations of some or all of the following elements: instructional resources; instructional media; learning skills development; tutoring and instructional development" (p. 2). Such an amalgamation screens more institutions in than out of the group designated as having learning centers. Yet his basic finding is solid; substantial numbers of postsecondary institutions have learning centers. Among public institutions in the United States 75 percent of the four-year institutions and 57 percent of the two-year institutions have learning centers; among private institutions 38 percent of the four-year institutions and 23 percent of the two-year institutions have learning centers (Sullivan, 1979). Beyond the obvious fact that learning centers abound, these data speak to the enormous diversity of learning center programs. What would the LAPs at Stanford, Berkeley, and Harvard have in common with those at Ricks College, Bluefield State College, and Kankakee Community College? The definitional problem is overwhelming. What then is a LAP? I hypothesize that this term is now used to cover products of the last two decades of development and innovation in the collegiate world. These include aspects of the learning resources center movement, the instructional technology movement, and underlying all these aspects of the egalitarian movements of the fifties, sixties, and seventies that saw a shift toward more open admissions across higher education. Add light leavenings of federally funded student assistance programs and faculty development projects, and we approach a description of the LAP as a national phenomenon. Now does that matter? And how does that relate to evaluation methodologies?

The LAP does not have a single definition or function that can be stated and applied. A LAP is not part of a unified movement with agreed-upon goals and standards; it is what it is in a particular institution at a particular time. This means that we can not be sure what it is we are

attempting to evaluate until a specific program is described and identified within its context. And this makes a great deal of difference in the approach to evaluation. At the most basic level, a LAP is not an entity with concrete qualities and functions; rather it is a phenomenon resulting from perceptions of the purpose of the institution and the interests of members of the institution.

LAP, therefore, may differ in purposes, methods, and reporting patterns as much within institutions as between institutions. No doubt there are clusters of institutions with similar programs, but clustering would not be related to similar size or funding pattern as much as it would be related to common missions and orientations as expressed in admissions policies, living patterns, and curricular orientations. LAP are profoundly different one from another; we do not really know what they are generically, and whatever they are, they are more than one thing.

Evaluation

Because evaluation is an emerging and changing field, definitions are in a state of flux. Early concepts of evaluation stressed a model borrowed from the natural sciences. In this scientific model, measurable goals were established for programs, and evaluation consisted of measurements of attainment against the stated goals. These models assumed that goals were known and agreed upon and that measurement of progress toward those goals was possible. Implicit in this scientific model was and is the belief that "truth" is what can be stated and measured and that this truth is the proper stuff of evaluation.

Later workers in evaluation have proposed alternative models that allow us to consider different forms of truth. A major alternative to the scientific model is the process evaluation model, which concentrates upon evaluation as a process that occurs within a specific setting—a setting that itself influences the goals and the results of the evaluation. The Stufflebeam context, input, process, and product (CIPP) model fits this pattern while Scriven's goal-free model goes even further and advocates evaluation without preset goals. In this model, the actual effects of the program are identified, and an effort is made to relate these effects to actual needs of the program recipients. Here the emphasis is upon the emergent truth appropriate for the program. Increasingly the assumption that we can anticipate the outcomes of programs and design measurements for those outcomes is being challenged, and alternative models are being proposed that allow the activities of the program itself to influence (Stufflebeam) or determine (Scriven) the characteristics and effects of the programs that are considered in evaluation.

Evaluation, then, is not a single concept. Cronbach (1980, p. 14) defines evaluation as "systematic examination of events occurring in and consequent on a contemporary program—an examination conducted to assist in improving this program and other programs having the same general purpose." Guba and Lincoln (1981) take a much more restricted view. They view each program to be evaluated as a unique event with special characteristics derived from the purposes of the audience that requested the evaluation, the context of the program itself, and the perceptions of the various actors within the program: "The major purpose of evaluation we define as responding to an audience's requirements for information, particularly in ways that take account of the several value perspectives of its members" (p. 36). They go on to distinguish evaluations according to their formative or summative intent and their focus on general or local application of the program.

To conclude this point, let me cite the work of Earnest House, who identified eight different evaluation models (House, 1978). His models included all those identified here plus others; this supports the point that there is no one best way in evaluation; there are only appropriate ways. There is no one truth that is the stuff of evaluation today; there are only multiple forms of truth representing the pluralistic nature of our activities and interests. The task of evaluation is to find the appropriate form of evaluation for the task at hand.

Now where do we go from here? The LAP is not a single concept but a situationally defined phenomenon with many possible forms and functions. Evaluation is also a multifaceted phenomenon with many forms and almost as many functions. We have made a muddle. Is there a way out of this muddle? I think there is. When concepts whirl about without order, a useful approach is to arrange each concept in a meaningful way—to develop a taxonomy based upon some basic organizing construct and then search for order across the constructs. In other words, search for congruence between the patterns of LAP and the patterns of evaluations. If congruence can be found, there should be a logical and a practical relationship between the two concepts under study. In this case, there should be a logical and practical relationship between the types of LAP and the types of evaluations. We should, therefore, be able to classify particular programs and then be guided logically to identify the purposes behind the evaluation and the appropriate type of evaluation methodology for that program.

A Taxonomy of Learning Assistance Programs

Any classification scheme, or taxonomy, is only as valid as the number of variables it considers and as useful as the array of variables considered. This taxonomy proposes to use three arrays with a limited number of variables for each. From these three arrays, a basic classification scheme for LAP will be derived. LAP can be classified on three bases: their function, their form, and their context.

Function. The functions of LAP are best seen as a continuum anchored at one extreme by the program with the single purpose of remedying existing student academic deficiencies so each student can be successful in the institution's academic or mainstream curriculum. The other extreme of the continuum is anchored by programs that work as part of many components of the institution focusing on helping students develop their full academic and personal potentials through a variety of academic and nonacademic activities.

The first extreme I call the remedial model because it attempts to remedy the student's academic weakness before allowing the student into the mainstream of the curriculum. This model also has a strong quality control function as it operates to screen weak students out of the curriculum and only allows competent students to pass through and into the mainstream curriculum, thus protecting the academic quality of the institution. The other extreme I call the developmental model because its primary purpose is to encourage the development of the student as a total person. This model's concern for academic quality is matched or exceeded by concern for providing equality of opportunity to all students. This equality may be seen as an equal opportunity to share in the academic opportunities of college life, in the social and growth opportunities of college life, or in the advantages that accrue through the various forms of certification associated with the college experience. These remedial and developmental functions of programs have been addressed elsewhere by Cross (1976), Roueche and Snow (1977), and most directly by Clowes (1979, 1980) so they will not be expanded on here.

The first array of variables, then, is about function. A LAP with a primarily remedial function would stress its screening role for the mainstream curriculum; it also would represent a barrier to full admission to that curriculum. Remedially oriented programs would work with students on their basic skills of reading, writing, mathematics, and perhaps study skills. The program emphasis would be academic, and the expectation would be that the student would provide the motivation necessary to master the skills presented. This function might be evidenced in specific performance criteria in basic skills areas or specified rates of progress to maintain eligibility for the remedial programs. The remedial programs would be seen as a means to support the academic curriculum and not as an end in themselves.

A program with a primarily developmental function would stress the support role of the LAP as it operated to sustain students in the college environment. Developmentally oriented programs would work with students on improving decision-making skills, making career and personal choices, developing self-assessment skills, and improving basic skills. Study skills would be stressed within a counseling-oriented and strongly supportive environment. The LAP would attend to motivation and assist the student in developing and maintaining the motivation needed to continue profitably in the program and to move into the mainstream curriculum if that became appropriate. These programs might be seen as ends in themselves since they provide important services to a special population of students not otherwise served by the institution. Program functions can be classified into the two extreme models—remedial or developmental—or will fall somewhere within the extremes as a mixed model. This is represented in Figure 1.

Figure 1. Array of Functions

Agreement of knowledgeable informants		remedial	developmental
about assignment on the		mixed	mixed

Agreement of knowledgeable informants about assignment on the continuum — High / Low

Remedial   Developmental

Continuum of functions from remedial to developmental

Form. The second array of variables concerns form. The form a program takes represents the way it has developed over time, either in a planned or serendipitous manner. While function can be influenced by internal and external political concerns, the actual form that develops to make the LAP work often more clearly represents the realities of the program. No continuity is necessary between the stated functions of the program and the actual form it takes; in fact, discontinuity may be the more normal state. Therefore, attention to the actual form of a program is important. Clowes (1979) has constructed an ideal model for basic skills programs that identifies specific programmatic forms with the remedial and the developmental functions. These programmatic forms can be arrayed along a similar continuum from remedial to developmental to allow a comparison with the array by function.

LAPs with a high convergence of form at the remedial end of the continuum would have the following characteristics: the program would present basic skills classwork through the traditional academic departments although usually with a remedial course designation. The courses would have narrow foci on specific skills development. These courses and other services would be seen as supportive of the mainstream curriculum and would operate to supplement the regular academic program, not to replace it for the basic skills student. Enrollment in basic skills courses or attendance at support laboratories or learning centers would be voluntary.

Faculty or counselors might refer students to a learning center or basic skills class, but the motivation for attendance would have to come from the student. Testing for basic skills levels would be done by individual academic faculty in their classrooms and would not be binding on the student. The form of instruction in such a remedially oriented program would be an effort dominated by academic area teachers with some support from the counseling staff. Instruction would be presented in departmentally sponsored noncredit courses and through support laboratories or learning assistance centers organized along departmental lines. For example, the English Department would teach basic English courses and run the writing lab. Individualized and self-paced instruction would be a common aspect of these programs, especially in the laboratory settings. In this model, the LAP is more apt to be a loose federation of courses, learning centers/labs, and activities, with a diffused pattern of responsibility.

LAPs with a high convergence of form toward the developmental end of the continuum would have a different pattern. A program whose form indicated a focus on the development of the total person and an emphasis upon providing equality of opportunity would more probably present a fully integrated program designed to serve the deficient student, not just a series of courses and labs. This effort would be a program organized as a threshold over which all students must pass in order to enter the mainstream curriculum of the college. Institution-wide testing would be required, and while the academically prepared student would pass directly over the threshold into the main curriculum, the academically deficient student would be required to enter the developmental program and demonstrate success there before entering the mainstream curriculum. These programs would be dominated by counselors or counseling-oriented faculty and would be classroom-based with few support labs and individualized instruction. The classroom-based work would typically carry academic credit either through the traditional department structure or through specially created interdisciplinary units established to administer the program. These programs would typically operate as a unified whole with a clear organizational structure, a separate faculty, and planned coordination with the other student support activities on the campus.

A classification scheme for LAPs can be developed on the form of the program. The variables used would be whether the program is a loose federation of courses in specific skills and related activities or a full program for the deficient student; whether it is a support or threshold program; whether participation is voluntary or required; whether testing is course by course and optional or institution-wide and mandatory; whether the program is dominated by academicians or by counseling-oriented faculty; whether it is lab/learning center-based or classroom-based; and whether activities are primarily noncredit or credit. LAPs can be classified by form to fit either the remedial or developmental pattern or to be mixed models with various combinations of these characteristics as represented in Figure 2.

Figure 2. Array of Form

Agreement of knowledgeable informants about assignment on the continuum		remedial	developmental
	High	remedial	developmental
	Low	mixed	mixed
		Remedial	Developmental

continuum of form from remedial
to developmental

Context. The third array of variables involves the context of the LAP. Context is the internal and external environment of the program. The internal environment is made up of the students and staff, their perceptions of themselves, their roles, and of the LAP. The external environment, consists of the institution within which the program operates, significant others' perceptions of its role, and its formally assigned roles and resources.

Clark Kerr (1963) made a useful distinction among institutions of higher education that relates to this use of context. He distinguished between institutions involved in knowledge production and operating on a quality/excellence model and those whose primary role was providing access to higher education through a need/access model. I believe Kerr was distinguishing between the institutions that stress the production of knowledge and the transmission of the traditions and knowledge of the society and the institutions whose primary role is providing citizens with the training, general education, and preparation for upward mobility in the society—a role that is essential if the society is to continue to grow through the utilization of knowledge. Kerr envisioned a pluralistic society developing a pluralism in higher education. I believe this relates to the contexts within which we and our LAPs operate.

Earlier I asked how we could expect to find commonality across sets of research universities, comprehensive four-year institutions, and a series of two-year institutions. In my more naive moments, I like to imagine that the type of institution will allow us to find commonalities, but that is not so. There appear to be as many differences within types of institutions as there are across types. If we cannot look to the type of institution for commonality, where can we look? If research universities differ among themselves as much as they do from public community colleges, where can we look? I think Kerr's distinction is a good beginning point.

Kerr helps with the question of context because he starts us looking in the right places. What does the institution think is its function? All institutions—from the research university to the local community college—claim to be producing knowledge and performing the traditional elitist academic goals to some degree. But what is the dominant context within which the institution works? What are the dominant expectations of the faculty—publishing, research, or service? Is the admissions policy a rigid quality control device, a flexible blend to get the best quality possible but still fill the freshman classes, or an aggressively pursued open door? Is the institutional stress on student attainment of traditional academic values and skills, upon the acquisition of marketable skills, upon the establishing of a particular world or religious view? These characteristics and others equally nebulous make up a strong ingredient acting upon any program within an institution. Yes, research universities have LAPs, but their tasks are very different from the tasks of a LAP at an open-door, urban, nonresidential four-year institution serving a minority population. Yes, community colleges have LAPs and logically should pursue a developmental model. But many see their role as fine tuning the open door and maintaining academic standards even though—and sometimes because—they are at the extreme edge of the open admissions spectrum. And yes, we all know respectable four-year residential liberal arts institutions that operate with a virtually open door but through nurture and prodding, through a blend of a remedially oriented academic component and a developmentally oriented student life and resident program, manage to produce graduates who are a source of pride some four or five years later.

Again a muddle exists out there, but again a modest classification scheme can come to our aid. Contexts can be classified then as either representing Kerr's quality/excellence model or his needs/access model, as either a quality or opportunity oriented context, or as in our terms either a remedially or developmentally oriented context.

Figure 3. Array of Context

Agreement of knowledgeable informants about assignment on the continuum		(quality) Remedial	(opportunity) Developmental
	High	Remedial	Developmental
	Low	Mixed	Mixed
		Remedial	Developmental

Continuum of Context from
remedial to developmental

I have made the argument that LAPs can be classified by function, form, and context. In each case, a specific program may be assigned clearly as either remedial, developmental, or mixed. With some precision, one may assign a mixed model more to one end of the continuum than to another. This process can be performed on each program in three ways, thus allowing a clear classification to emerge.

A Taxonomy of Evaluation Methods

At the beginning of this chapter, I encouraged you with the notion that we could first classify LAPs, then evaluation methods, and finally find congruence between the two that would illuminate our thinking about the appropriate evaluation models for a specific program. Now that I have proposed a classification scheme for LAPs, it is time to look at evaluation methods.

Theoretical Distinctions Among Models. Several experts in evaluation have been laboring to bring order out of the current state of near chaos in that field. At the risk of oversimplifying, I would like to draw on the careful and intricate work of three writers to develop a classification scheme of evaluation methods.

As mentioned earlier, Earnest House (1978) identified eight evaluation models currently in use today. Guba and Lincoln (1981) propose that there are really only two major types of evaluation models. They consider that the early goals-oriented evaluation models of Tyler and Popham, and House's first two models, are really one major type, which they call the countenance evaluation model. This model assumes that goals are known and that the purpose of evaluation is to determine how well the predetermined goals are being met. This model implies that some program improvement goals can be met while focusing primarily on how well the program actually meets it original planned outcomes, that formative and summative evaluation can be accomplished at the same time.

Guba and Lincoln's other type of evaluation model, which includes the remaining six models identified by House, is the responsive evaluation model. They see responsive evaluation as "a process for describing an evaluand and judging its merit and worth" (1981, p. 35). Here "merit" is used to describe an intrinsic quality of the entity being evaluated, the evaluance, which might be established by measurement against an outside objective standard or by comparison with other entities of established merit. "Worth" is an extrinsic quality of the evaluand, relating to how it affects or relates to its environment. The criteria for determinations of worth might be measurement of outcomes of the LAP against identified needs of the clients or against the perceived needs of the clients as identified by significant others in the organization.

Guba's basic point is that the countenance model for evaluation takes an unrealistic view of the world. This model assumes we know what we are attempting to do and how to do it, and that there is consensus within the organization on all these points. This just is not so in the real world, although it is so in the world of the controlled scientific experiment from which this model was derived. The responsive model allows for the uncertainty of goals and means to achieve these goals because it attends in various ways to the process of establishing goals, accommodating uncertainty, and attempting to find usable components of reality. Guba then draws the connection to evaluation methodology through a representation of earlier work by Willems and Rausch (1969). When it is possible to impose tight controls on the outcomes of a program and on the conditions or activities within a program, the traditional methods of scientific inquiry are appropriate. This would be the domain of countenance models of evaluation. However, when there is little control over either outcomes of a program or of the conditions or activities within, then a responsive evaluation model is appropriate. In the extreme case, the pure form of responsive evaluation—naturalistic inquiry—would be appropriate. When either controls over outcomes or controls over conditions and activities are low, then one of the more goal-oriented forms of responsive evaluation (alone or in combination with countenance evaluation) would be appropriate. This is represented in Figure 4.

Figure 4. Ideal Evaluation Models

Control over outcomes of the program			
	High	Mixed	"Ideal" experiment
	Low	"Ideal" naturalistic inquiry	Mixed
		Low	High

Control over conditions and activities
of the program

Source: Adapted from Guba and Lincoln, 1981, p. 79.

Since we demonstrated earlier that there is little consensus about the nature of LAPs or about the process of evaluation, Guba's point about the inappropriateness of countenance evaluation models seems particularly important. Traditional evaluations attempt to operate from known or agreed-upon goals and do a quantitative assessment of progress toward these goals. This is the "ideal" scientific inquiry, but it is inappropriate to most LAPs. Responsive evaluation—especially in its extreme form of naturalistic inquiry—does not require controls over the outcomes or conditions and activities of the program because it accommodates itself to these realities. Naturalistic inquiry attends to questions of worth, or value within the context of that program with its unique audience and context. Questions of merit, the innate value of the program, are not answered but are also not appropriate questions for most LAPs.

Responsive evaluation consists of information gathering through questionnaire, interview, observation, and the use of archival data. In these approaches, the evaluator is an active part of the process through assessment of data received, redirecting of the inquiry, and the constant feedback into the process. In this sense, responsive evaluation shapes the goals of the evaluation effort rather than being shaped by prior goals. The important point is to recognize that each type of responsive evaluation is appropriate to situations with different degrees of control over outcomes and the program activities. How best can we evaluate a LAP when it is such a buzz of activities and people? Not through acting as if we had high levels of control if we do not, but through choosing a model that fits our reality.

Patton (1980) went one step further and proposed that House's eight evaluation models could be correlated with the appropriate methodology. He argued that the countenance models could only be addressed through quantitative analysis. However, some evaluation models were approachable using a combination of quantitative and nonquantitative methodologies while others were best approached using only the nonquantitative models. This is precisely the point represented in Figure 4.

Practical Distinctions in the Nature of Truth. Evaluation has come a long way from when it was seen as providing the final answer. Today it concerns itself as much with trying to identify the appropriate question. Evaluation in a pluralistic society is a complex but fascinating phenomenon. Lily Tomlin is quoted as saying, "Lady, I do not make up things. That is lies. Lies is not true. But the truth could be made up if you knew how. And that's the truth" (Patton, 1980, p. 269). We must consider the matter Lily Tomlin raises in order to make proper choices about evaluation methods.

A real question that must be addressed is what kind of truth are we after in a particular evaluation effort. We can create different truths— different types of answers or information—depending upon the method we choose as our evaluation technique. Martha Maxwell (1979) says we should design evaluations of LAPs for administrators and thus provide them the kinds of truth they want and we want them to have. This is probably good practical advice, and it can be accommodated properly within the Stufflebeam CIPP model. However, there is a broader question lurking beneath the surface. What kind of truth do we want to reveal? Guba and Lincoln (1981) suggest we must distinguish between considerations of merit and worth. These were distinguished earlier, but the basic thrust is important. If we are considering the merit of a program, we are considering its intrinsic worth. This assumes that we can assess the LAP as an objective entity that contains within itself all the elements necessary for its evaluation. The criteria for evaluation are also assumed to be objective and known. If we are considering the worth of a program, we are looking at extrinsic values that relate more to a local and practical phenomenon with criteria for evaluation related to the specific purposes, environment, and actors of that single program. These are two different types of truth statements. Statements of merit have a connotation of objectivity and generalizability; statements of worth have a connotation of subjectivity and particularism.

Another consideration in the type of truth statement desired is the standard distinction between evaluations designed to produce formative information and those designed to produce summative information. Here we distinguish between information for the improvement or changing of programs, usually gathered for the actual program actors (formative), and information designed to assess the actual accomplishments of a specific programs, usually gathered for both the program actors and the administrators within the larger organization (summative). Figure 5 displays this graphically and includes reference to the type of evaluation methods generally associated with each.

Figure 5. Evaluation Methods Related to Truth Statements

	Formative	Summative
Merit	Mixed	Quantitative
Worth	Qualitative	Mixed

The underlying assumption is that quantitative methods are appropriate in situations where the criteria for the evaluation are clear and have some general credence. Also, the quantitative methods have more direct relevance to evaluation aimed at establishing the final outcomes of a program and its specific accomplishments as opposed to concerns for process and the development of alternative goals or activities. Qualitative methods are presented as most appropriate in relating to local and unique programs and particularly to shaping their goals and activities. The many cases that fall between the extremes would be best served by a mix of methods.

Practical Distinctions on the Nature of Information. The kinds of information available and the kinds desired as products of the evaluation are important considerations in choosing an appropriate method. Information available to assist in program evaluation can be classified from "hard" to "soft" information. Hard data, both specific and comparative, would be counts of student utilization of a facility or progress made in specific skill improvement, as assessed through pretest/posttest designs and through measures of student persistence in the LAP activities, in the mainstream curriculum, and through to graduation. Soft data would be student reports of their learning experiences, faculty impressions, perceptions of significant others, observation and process reports by trained observors, subjective assessments of student changes in attitude and in performance, and so forth. A basic distinction would be that hard data would be objective data and soft data would be based on perceptions. Where hard data are available and used in the evaluation, quantitative methodologies would be appropriate in either the pure or mixed form. When soft data are the primary type available, qualitative methodology would be appropriate.

The kind of information desired as a product also determines the method of evaluation. If in-depth information about a single program, a program component, or a limited number of subjects is desired, then qualitative methodologies are the appropriate tool. Thus, if depth is the desired characteristic of the information to be gathered, then qualitative methodology is the methodology of choice. As Patton (1980, p. 67) puts it, "Qualitative methods permit the evaluator to study selected issues in depth and detail; the fact that data collection is not constrained by predetermined categories of analysis contributes to the depth and detail of qualitative data." However, if breadth of information is desired, quantitative methods are more appropriate. Quantitative methods limit the response categories to a few predetermined and standardized options. This allows the evaluator to "measure the reactions of many subjects to a limited set of questions, thus facilitating comparison and statistical aggregation of the data" (p. 98). These relationships are expressed in Figure 6.

Figure 6. Evaluation Methods Related to Information Available and to Information Desired

Information Available	Hard	Mixed	Quantitative
	Soft	Qualitative	Mixed
		Depth	Breadth

Information Desired

In this section, a taxonomy of evaluation methods has been proposed on three bases: on the basis of theoretical models, on the nature of the truth statements desired, and on the basis of the information available and desired. Each of these classification schemes allows the evaluator to identify an appropriate evaluation method along a continuum from scientific inquiry or quantitative methods through mixed methods at one end of the continuum to naturalistic inquiry or qualitative methods at the other end. The opportunity to identify an appropriate methodology on three bases allows the evaluator to decide which basis is most important for the particular study or to apply all three and determine which method is the most appropriate overall.

Conclusion

A muddle exists in the concepts of both LAPs and of evaluation. To assist in reducing the muddle, this chapter provides a series of classification schemes for LAPs, for evaluation models, and for evaluation methods. LAPs can be classified on the basis of their function, their form, and their context. The results of these classifications can be drawn together to gain an insight into the nature of the program to be evaluated. Then the models of evaluation are classified such that LAPs can be related to them and the appropriate evaluation model identified. Next, distinctions are drawn among evaluation methods on two practical considerations with the idea that these considerations can also be related back to the earlier classifications of LAPs. The concept of congruence is offered as the basis for asserting that the classifications of LAPs and of evaluation models and methods have a logical and reasonable relationship. This pattern of analysis can help free those working to evaluate LAPs from the rigid tyranny of the existing goal-oriented evaluation models as the only appropriate models. Perhaps it will open them to consider the numerous other options practically and logically available.

References

Christ, F. L. "Systems for Learning Assistance: Learners, Learning Facilitators, and Learning Centers." In F. L. Christ (Ed.), *Interdisciplinary Aspects of Reading Instruction*. Proceedings of the Fourth Annual Conference of the Western College Reading Asociation, 1971.

Clowes, D. A. "Form and Function." *Journal of Developmntal and Remedial Education*, 1979, 3 (*1*), 2, 3, 13.

Clowes, D. A. "More Than a Definitional Problem: Remedial, Compensatory, and Developmental Education." *Journal of Developmental and Remedial Education*, 1980, 4 (*1*), 8–10.

Cronbach, L. J., and others. *Toward Reform of Program Evaluation: Aims, Methods, and Institutional Arrangements*. San Francisco: Jossey-Bass, 1980.

Cross, K. P. *Accent on Learning: Improving Instruction and Reshaping the Curriculum*. San Francisco: Jossey-Bass, 1976.

Guba, E. G., and Lincoln, Y. S. *Effective Evaluation: Improving the Usefulness of Evaluation Results Through Responsive and Naturalistic Approaches*. San Francisco: Jossey-Bass, 1981.

House, E. R. "Assumptions Underlying Evaluation Models." *Educational Researcher*, 1978, 7, 4–12.

Kerr, C. *The Uses of the University*. Cambridge, Mass.: Harvard University Press, 1963.

Maxwell, M. *Improving Student Learning Skills: A Comprehensive Guide to Successful Practices and Programs for Increasing the Performance of Underprepared Students*. San Francisco: Jossey-Bass, 1979.

Patton, M. Q. *Qualitative Evaluation Methods*. Beverly Hills, Calif.: Sage, 1980.

Roueche, J. E., and Snow, J. J. *Overcoming Learning Problems: A Guide to Developmental Education in College*. San Francisco: Jossey-Bass, 1977.

Sullivan, L. L. *Sullivan's Guide to Learning Centers in Higher Education*. Portsmouth, N.H.: Entelek, 1979.

Willems, E. P., and Rausch, H. L. *Naturalistic Viewpoints in Psychological Research*. New York: Holt, Rinehart and Winston, 1969.

Darrel A. Clowes is an associate professor of curriculum and community college education at Virginia Polytechnic Institute and State University. He has taught previously at Jefferson Community College, Auburn University, and the University of Texas and held administrative positions with Miami Dade Community College and the U.S. Peace Corps/Korea. He holds degrees in philosophy/comparative literature from Dartmouth College, in English from Oberlin College, and in education from the University of Texas at Austin.

Traditional evaluation that focuses on process and product will not suffice for the learning assistance programs of the 1980s.

Role and Scope of Evaluation

Robert L. Moore

Evaluation of learning assistance programs has traditionally focused on product (the end results) and process (the means to attain these results). Evaluators have borrowed familiar methodology and have applied techniques that have proven effective in social science applications and other educational settings.

Many of these familiar methodologies can be categorized into the following ten evaluation frameworks: experimental research designs, quasi-experimental research designs, professional judgment, measurement methods, congruency comparison, cost-effectiveness approaches, behavioral taxonomies, systems analyses, informal evaluation, and goal-free/responsive evaluation.

These frameworks were suggested primarily by Alkin and Fitz-Gibbon (1975), Arnn and Strickland (1975), Campbell and Stanley (1966), Gardner (1977), Graham (1976), Land (1976), Rosenthal (1976), Scriven (1974), Stake (1967), Steinaker and Bell (1976), Stufflebeam (1974), and Stufflebeam and others, (1971). Each has value for learning assistance evaluation to the extent to which it assesses the worth as defined by social utility (Worthen and Sanders, 1973) or the extent to which the evaluation can contribute to making "judgments about the worth of a program or elements of a program" (Brown, 1980, p. 76).

C. C. Walvekar (Ed.), *New Directions for College Learning Assistance: Assessment of Learning Assistance Services*, no. 5. San Francisco: Jossey-Bass, 1981.

The suggested frameworks contribute to "judgments about worth" in varying degrees. Some are quite narrow and rigorous (experimental and quasi-experimental designs); others take a broader, less rigorous view (professional judgment, goal-free/responsive evaluations). Further, within the various frameworks, a wide variety of philosophical bases, rationales, time frames, techniques, instrumentation, audiences, reporting methods, and system feedback are employed. All can be and have proven to be useful.

However, the focus of these frameworks for evaluation is primarily on product and process: What is being attained and how effective or efficient is the program in delivering these attainments?

The primary focus on product and process leads to potential problems, particularly when applied to learning assistance programs at institutions with changing populations, ever-shrinking operating budgets, political pressures, and a growing uneasiness about their "fit" in the larger, societal mission (which can, it seems, change nearly overnight—consider the large influx of unemployed auto workers into financially strapped Michigan colleges).

Program evaluations that focus only on product and process tend to be self-serving, myopic, and largely unresponsive. They are self-serving to the extent that they defend and protect the program and focus on getting "a larger share of the pie." They are myopic to the extent that they do not view the larger administrative, political, and financial constraints within the institution. And they are unresponsive to the extent that they do not take into account the growing economic forces, shifting political pressures, ever-changing needs of a diverse student population, and redefined institutional missions.

The central theme of this chapter is that an evaluation framework is needed that is comprehensive enough to go beyond product and process. The framework must broadly encompass institutional need and specifically take into account the ever-changing environmental milieu within which the learning assistance program, of necessity, operates.

Capabilities and Limitations of Evaluation Frameworks

Experimental Research Designs. Campbell and Stanley (1966) considered only three designs to be "true" experimental research designs. These designs (numbered four, five, and six in their publication) ensured both internal and external validity and reliability through random assignment of subjects to the treatment settings, careful comparison of matched (natural or statistical) groups, and a sufficient number of things to be measured for statistical analysis. Where conditions of randomization, comparable groups, or sufficient number cannot be met, true experimental research designs may yield questionable findings. Often, no practical or economic way exists to conduct true experiments in learning assistance programs whereby "variables are manipulated and their effects on other variables observed" (p. 1).

Quasi-Experimental Research Designs. When "(the researcher) lacks the full control over the scheduling of experimental stimuli . . . such situations can be regarded as quasi-experimental designs" (Campbell and Stanley, 1966, p. 34). However, "because full experimental control is lacking, it becomes imperative that the researcher be thoroughly aware of which specific variables his particular design fails to control" (p. 34).

Campbell and Stanley cite ten designs that they classify as quasi-experimental: time-series, equivalent-time samples, equivalent-materials samples, nonequivalent control groups, counterbalanced, separate-sample pretest-posttest, separate-sample pretest-posttest control group, multiple time-series, institutional cycle, and regression discontinuity. The reader is referred to the source for a full treatment of these designs, including cautions regarding their use.

The designs listed offer sufficient latitude that one or more might be used to evaluate selected portions of a learning assistance program. However, a broad evaluation of a program would be difficult using quasi-experimental designs, due to the same lack of control problems inherent in true experimental designs.

Professional Judgment. Evaluation within the professional judgment framework includes "structured visitation by peers" (Stake, 1967, p. 523), panel studies in "interview waves" (Campbell and Stanley, 1966, p. 68), and "a qualified professional . . . asked to examine the thing to be evaluated and then render an expert opinion regarding its quality, effectiveness, or efficiency" (Gardner, 1977, p. 574).

When professional judgment is applied, "the resulting statement of relative worth is the evaluation" (p. 574). Since the expertise of the judge(s) is relied upon as a basic assumption in professional judgment, criteria, checklists, and values may or may not be explicitly detailed. The judge is assumed to have "superior knowledge which accompanies stature in the particular field in question" (p. 575).

Examples of the use of professional judgment include accreditation teams, doctoral committees, peer review of grant proposals, referees for selection of manuscripts for publication, and faculty committees for promotion and tenure decisions (Gardner, 1977; Stufflebeam and others, 1971; Worthen and Sanders, 1973).

The advantages of professional judgment are that it is "easily implemented, uses (the) assimilative and integrative capabilities of human intellect, and recognizes outstanding expertise" (Gardner, 1977, p. 587). The disadvantages that characterize professional judgment are that "results (are) criticized as nonreplicable, noncomparable, and overly subjective, and generalizability is thus difficult or impossible" (p. 587).

Measurement Methods. Measurement methods are described as the standardized "measurement of results, effects, or performance, using some type of formal instrument" (Gardner, 1977, p. 587). It is assumed that the "phenomena to be measured have significant measureable attributes, and that instruments exist (or can be designed) which are capable of measuring them" (p. 576). The commonly accepted practice of using standard instruments where possible has led to ease of replication and thus generalizability. Measurement is among the oldest and most widely practiced educational activities; it is also widely misused, particularly in higher education (Gardner, 1977).

Examples of the use of measurement methods include standardized testing (for example, SAT, ACT, Nelson-Denny Reading, Brown-Holtzman Survey of Study Skills, Habits, and Attitudes), attitude surveys, teaching effectiveness questionnaires, and faculty activity questionnaires.

Advantages of the measurement method of evaluation have been summarized by Gardner (1977): proper validation and consistent application results in high comparability and replicability; the data are mathematically manipulable; and the results are generalizable. Disadvantages are also cited by Gardner: many variables are difficult or impossible to measure; measureable attributes are often irrelevant; and, in general, the technique is often inappropriate and/or inflexible, serving more the method than the phenomena under evaluation.

Congruency Comparison. Congruency comparison involves examining the intents of a program, observing the actual happenings, and recording the differences (Stake, 1967). "The data are congruent if what was intended actually happened. To be fully congruent, the intended antecedents, transactions, and outcomes would have to come to pass" (p. 532). Stake pointed out that "congruence does not indicate that outcomes are reliable or valid, but that what was intended did occur" (p. 534).

Stake suggested two methods of judging the worth of a program using a congruency framework: (1) with respect to absolute standards of excellence as reflected by personal judgments and (2) with respect to relative standards of excellence as reflected by characteristics of alternate programs. The evaluator must choose (judge) which standards of excellence have the greatest influence for the decision at hand. Comparing characteristics of alternate programs involves choosing the proper referent programs and determining to which characteristics one should attend.

Since a strong goal orientation exists in congruency comparison, this evaluation framework is attractive for competency-based programs and measurement of program success in meeting broader goals and objectives. Comparing student outcomes against stated behavioral objectives or learning contracts is a straightforward congruency process.

Congruency observations, comparisons, and judgments are replicable and generalizable. Provus (1971), Scriven (1967), and Stake (1967) have contributed to model and theory building in congruency frameworks. Advantages of congruency comparisons are summarized by Gardner (1977) as providing an objective basis for evaluation, preestablishing judgment criteria, and pertaining to current societal concerns. Disadvantages cited by Gardner are that the focus may be too limited, not all worthy goals are easily identified, important side effects may be overlooked, and there is an overemphasis on evaluation of the end product (summative) at the expense of the process (formative).

Cost-Effectiveness Approaches. Land (1976, pp. 95–96) identified a problem-statement classification as a useful way to approach cost-effective evaluation:

- *Problem of estimation:* forecasting the costs and benefits of a proposed program over its expected lifetime
- *Investment decision problem:* comparing the trade-off between the chosen project and alternate investments
- *Problem of measuring achievement:* monitoring program operation to compare estimated costs and benefits with actual costs incurred and benefits received
- *Cost allocation problem:* allocating development, operating, and benefit costs to the appropriate users
- *Program control problem:* controlling the development process with respect to its use of time and resources.

Land borrowed the classification scheme from industry and applied it to educational settings.

PPBS (Program, Planning, and Budgeting System), PERT (Program Evaluation Review Technique), CPM (Critical Path Method), operations research, and systems analysis have been suggested as methods that may employ cost-effectiveness evaluation measures (Carss, 1969; Haller, 1974; Heath and Orlich, 1977; Hill, 1972).

Advantages of cost-effectiveness evaluation approaches are the emphasis on efficiency and effectiveness, the provision of audit trails for accountability, the allocation of resources and time to the proper beneficiaries, and the provision of evaluation data in terms of a comparable commodity cost. Disadvantages are that time pressures often force a short-cutting of cost estimation parameters and that a tendency exists to restrict measures of benefit to only those elements which are directly observable and which will lead to cost reduction or cost avoidance (Land, 1976).

Behavioral Taxonomies. Steinaker and Bell (1976, p. 26) stated that "any effective taxonomy of educational objectives presupposes and possesses an intrinsic and functional evaluation system." The authors described evaluation under a taxonomy framework as containing two major elements: macro- and micro-evaluation. Macro-evaluation is an overall sequence of activities "with attendant strategies to provide perspective, direction, and feedback . . . as a basis for decisions in educational policy; in effect, an overall design" (p. 26). Micro-evaluation is a "strategy or strategies to measure results of individual or singular classroom activities and experiences; or said another way, a specific classroom-oriented design" (p. 26). Utilizing behavioral taxonomies as the basis of evaluation, an evaluation practitioner maps the strategies and activities stated or implied in the macro- and micro-levels of the behavioral taxonomy into evaluation strategies and activities on a one-to-one basis.

The inclusion of behavior taxonomy evaluation was provided for completeness of methodologies utilized to gather information for decision making in educational settings. But since the technique is clearly related to student learning activities, primarily in classroom situations, it is not fully appropriate as an evaluation framework to assess the overall worth of a program of learning assistance.

Systems Analyses. Evaluation under a systems analysis framework may be characterized as the "feedback loops" of the stages of program definition, design, development, installation, operation, and support. Thus, system evaluation is continuously both formative and summative. When program implementation proceeds in such a manner, particularly if decision makers, technical personnel, and users team together to judge the merit of each stage of activity, the final product is likely to be judged meritoriously.

Arnn and Strickland (1975) described a disadvantage of the systems approach: it often emphasizes nonhuman components at the expense of the people who will use the system. The authors described four "human system" difficulties. First, "systems approaches generally follow a problem-solving approach emphasizing steps and procedures but frequently ignoring the interaction of the people who are involved" (p. 14). They emphasized that it is people, not the system, who must find solutions to people-related problems. Second, dependence and apathy may arise unless the people in the system feel free to contribute to the process of choosing alternatives during the development process. Third, solution strategies that focus on system objectives may appear excellent on paper but fail to produce the desired results. Such failure may be due to the "same obstacles which prevented the success of old strategies; namely *person* obstacles. . . . If person obstacles are ignored, the system's chances for success may be limited" (p. 15). Fourth, persons responsible for the system (the "doers") and the users of the system (the "doees") may not have reached consensus on the goals of the system. "The consequence (of nonconsensus) may vary from apathy to mutiny, (but when) there is a consensus on the part of the doers and doees that the goals of the system are important, then all feel responsible for and work toward the attainment of these goals. . . . The direction of the system is internal (rather than external) in that all the participants value system goals and are willing to invest their time and efforts to work toward these goals" (p. 15).

Informal Evaluation. Intuitively, an informal evaluation framework exists when decision makers "evaluate" a program, process, product, or a system without benefit of an established evaluation framework. Such nonframework frameworks are common in education. Examples include the use of nonstandardized and nonvalidated instrumentation designed to measure the success of a program or attitudes of participants; the biased (nonrandom) sampling of learners; the reliance upon the judgment of participants with a vested (value) interest in the success of a program; and a "comparison with other events casually observed and remembered" (Campbell and Stanley, 1966, p. 6).

It does not necessarily follow that the persons responsible for an informal evaluation are attempting to "prove" the success of the program under evaluation, but such evaluation is characterized by a lack of external standards, little or no validity control, no attempt at generalizability to other settings, and, in general, a tendency to focus narrowly on certain, usually positive, aspects of the thing to be evaluated. Carrying such a procedure to its logical conclusion, even the output of an informal evaluation study might be screened to further focus on desirable components. An informal evaluation framework provides no structured impetus to objectively judge the merit of a program according to some systematic procedure.

Goal-Free/Responsive Evaluation. The notions of goal-free evaluation and responsive evaluation are closely related and have been combined here under one framework heading. Gardner (1977) has also treated the two under a single category. He calls goal-free evaluation "the critical examination of the institution, project, program, or thing irrespective of its goals" (p. 583).

According to Scriven (1974), attention to intended goals may actually get in the way of evaluation and prevent the discovery of important side effects: "The rhetoric of the original proposal (of a program) which had led to a particular product (is) frequently put forward as if it somehow (constitutes) supporting evidence for the excellence of the product. . . . Furthermore, the whole language of 'side effect' or 'secondary effect' or even 'unanticipated effect' . . . (is) used by evaluators to be a put-down of what might well be the crucial achievement. . . . Consideration and evaluation of goals (is) an unnecessary but also a possible contaminating step" (p. 35). Scriven pointed out that program goals are nearly always under- or overachieved so "why waste time rating the goals; which usually *are not* what is achieved" (p. 37).

Stufflebeam (1974) noted that Scriven had reversed his earlier notion of goal-based evaluation in favor of goal-free methodology. However, as early as 1967, Scriven hinted at evaluation without reference to goals: "Evaluation proper must include, as an equal partner with the measuring of performance against goals, procedures for the evaluation of the goals (themselves). *That is, if it is to have any reference to goals at all"* (Scriven, 1967, p. 52, emphasis added).

Later in the same paper, in distinguishing between formative and summative evaluators, Scriven observed that "evaluators . . . are handicapped so long as they are less than fully familiar with the subject matter being restructured, and less than fully sympathetic with the aims of the creative group. Yet once they become identified with those aims, emotionally as well as economically, they lose something of great importance to an objective evaluation—their independence. For this reason, the formative evaluators should, if at all possible, be distinguished from the summative evaluator, with whom they may certainly work in developing an acceptable summative evaluation schema, but formative evaluators should ideally *exclude* themselves from the role of judge in the summative evaluation" (p. 45, emphasis added).

In a more recent work, Scriven suggested the assignment of formative evaluation—with its attendant attention to the aims of the project—to a staff evaluator and the assignment of summative evaluation to an external evaluator who uses external standards of merit without reference to project goals. "The less the external evaluator hears about the goals of the project, the less tunnel vision will develop, the more attention will be paid to *looking* for actual effects (rather than *checking* on alleged effects)" (Scriven, 1974, p. 36, emphasis added).

Gardner has described "responsive evaluation" as proposed by Stake[1] in the following manner: "Responsive evaluation is an iterative process of acquiring information about an institution, program, or project; defining issues of importance to constituencies; and describing strengths and weaknesses relative to these issues" (Gardner, 1977, p. 583). Goals of the institution, program, or project carry no more weight with the evaluator than the processes, resources, products, or participants. Stake has been more explicit than Scriven in providing a guiding framework for evaluation in a goal-free/responsive manner. The following events, according to Stake, should be considered, not necessarily in sequence, but through a series of informal negotiations with constituencies:

- Talk with clients, staff, and audience
- Identify program scope
- Overview program activities
- Discover purposes and concerns
- Conceptualize issues and problems
- Identify data needs
- Select observers, judges, and informal instruments (if any)
- Observe selected antecedents, transactions, and outcomes

[1]The original source, unavailable to the present author, is an August 26, 1974, paper from Urbana, Illinois.

- "Thematize"—prepare portrayals and case studies
- Match issues to audiences
- Prepare and deliver presentations and formal reports (Gardner, 1977, p. 584).

Both Scriven's concept of goal-free evaluation and Stake's responsive evaluation framework place a high reliance on the skills of the evaluator. He or she must be able to recognize important relationships among program components, interact with people to elicit information, and interpret and convey decision-making information. The evaluator must think and perform holistically.

Advantages of goal-free/responsive evaluation are that it is flexible, adaptive, and useful in relatively unstructured situations; all processes, outcomes, resources, and objectives are potentially relevant; and it is a people- rather than system-oriented process and therefore has high acceptance potential (Gardner, 1977; see also Arnn and Strickland, 1975).

Disadvantages are that the unstructured nature of the evaluation may be difficult to focus and manage; results may be overly subjective and nonreplicable; and the evaluation outcome may be difficult to communicate to the intended audiences. Also, it cannot be ignored that goal-*based* evaluation is an accepted methodology, and audiences (administrators, for example) receiving goal-*free* evaluation results may have difficulty relating the findings to their own (usually broader) program goals.

Evaluation and Change

Braybrooke and Lindblom (1963) provide four categories of change that can be useful in establishing a baseline for a discussion of evaluation:

- *Homeostatic:* little or no change; evaluation is focused on quality control to ensure preservation of previously established standards and to restore status quo
- *Incremental:* continuous, developmental change; evaluation is focused on continuous, small improvements
- *Neomobilistic:* large, innovative change; evaluation is focused on inventing, testing, and diffusing solutions to significant problems
- *Metamorphic:* complete change; evaluation is focused on overarching theory to reach some utopian state.

Learning assistance programs could, at various times during their developmental history, fall into any one of the four change categories (even the metamorphic category if the utopian notion of equal educational opportunity for everyone through developmental, remedial, or compensatory learning assistance is accepted). However, most change will be in the incremental or neomobilistic categories in the learning assistance programs of the 1980s.

It is very probable that learning assistance programs will need to be responsive to shifting, diverse populations; sensitive to campus (and extra-campus) political forces; willing to demonstrate they are an integral part of the academic thrust of the institutions they serve; and accountable and cost-effective—if not revenue generating. To the extent that learning assistance programs retain students, revenue generation is realized through direct means, such as tuition and FTE allocations, and indirect means, such as the campus bookstore, auxiliary services, and so forth. Boylan (1978) has asserted that learning assistance programs are among the few campus units that have revenue-generating or "cost-benefit" potential. Learning assistance programs will be expected to improve (incrementally) at the very least and be ready for large (neomobilistic) change when called upon.

Evaluation as an Aid to Decision Making

An evaluation methodology that serves incremental and neomobilistic change is really answering decision-making questions as these changes are being made: Are there new populations to be served? Are there limits to the assistance to be given considering funding and staffing? Is program merger called for? Do components of the program require strengthening? Should parts be eliminated? Are institutional missions or federal guidelines changing, and, if so, what programming changes are required?

Clearly, an evaluation scheme that focuses primarily on product (attainments) and process (the means to attainment) may miss the broader issues inherent in the questions just posed, and decision making may be narrow and self-serving. Worse yet, short-range planning and decision making may result in a sacrifice of long-range effectiveness.

Evaluation must be ongoing (referred to in systems technology as continuous feedback), formative (aiding development and implementation), and summative (to determine the final worth of the program). However, before formative and summative decision-making stages are reached, a more pervasive evaluation of "fit" must be performed to aid decision making at the earliest possible point in program establishment. This evaluation must not be avoided, even if a workable program already exists. Also, a careful examination of the available human and nonhuman resources must be made to determine realistic implementation strategies.

An Evaluation Model to Serve Decision Making

Stufflebeam and others (1971) described an evaluation model that had been used primarily for large state, regional, and national projects, such as Tennessee Title III, Iowa State and Regional Data Processing

Centers, and the EPIC Evaluation Center in Tucson, Arizona. However, the theory and practice of evaluation described by these distinguished researchers lends itself well to the type of evaluation for decision making just described. Their synthesis model developed has been termed CIPP (context, input, process, and product). Even before one examines the model closely, it can be seen that product and process are included, but that two stages accompany (and actually precede) them: context and input.

A Decision-Making Evaluation Framework. According to Stufflebeam and others, "Educational evaluation is the process of delineating, obtaining, and providing useful information for judging decision alternatives" (p. 40). Key terms in the definition need to be highlighted for a better understanding of the framework:

- *Delineating* identifies information needed by specifying the decisions to be made and the criteria to be applied in weighing alternatives
- *Obtaining* is the making available of needed information through measurement, surveying, data processing, statistical analysis, and so forth
- *Providing* is the fitting together of collected information and then reporting it
- *Useful information* will be obtained for decision making if the proper alternatives and criteria are established
- *Process* as used in the definition implies the continuous, sequential, and iterative nature of decision making
- *Judging* is a key term in the definition. Evaluators have had differing viewpoints concerning judgment in the evaluation process. Scriven (1967) regarded evaluators who do not engage in the judging act as abrogating their role. Stake (1967) has stated that objectivity and credibility as an evaluator may be destroyed by participating in the decision-making (judging) process. Stufflebeam and others (1971, p. 43) were essentially in agreement with Stake's position, but preferred to consider a spectrum of evaluation/judging activity to avoid being caught on either horn of the dilemma.

Decision Types. Decisions regarding programs may be categorized into four types: planning decisions to determine program objectives, structuring decisions to design program procedures, implementing decisions to carry out program procedures, and recycling decisions to judge and react to final results. The Stufflebeam committee related these four decision types on a one-to-one basis with the four stages of the context, input, process, and product model.

Context Evaluation. The relevant environment within which a program is to operate is described in the context stage of the evaluation. Desired and actual conditions are described. Problems that exist to prevent desired conditions from being reached are identified. Strategies are identified to solve the problems. In other words, program objectives are stated in terms of a "fit" in the real world of desired conditions, impediments to reaching those conditions, and strategies that may be employed to overcome the impediments.

Input Evaluation. The needs, problems, and strategies identified through context evaluation compete with one another for the resources available to meet, solve, and implement them, respectively. At the end of an input evaluation stage, an assessment will be provided of one or more procedural designs in terms of costs and benefits. Among the criteria to be examined for each strategy are staffing requirements, time requirements, overall costs, outside assistance required, procedural barriers, existing resources, needed resources, campus support, facilities needed, data needed, and reporting requirements. In short, the program proposal is an outcome of the input stage of evaluation. The complexity of the proposal determined through input evaluation is largely a function of the needed changes in the program (determined during the context stage).

Process Evaluation. After a plan of action has been determined through the first two stages of evaluation, it is put in place and monitored through process evaluation. This stage of evaluation provides feedback with three major objectives: (1) to detect or predict defects in the procedural design(s) or implementation, (2) to provide information for programming (daily activities) decisions, and (3) to maintain a procedural record.

During the process stage of evaluation, successes and failures in procedure are documented. As the program progresses, a strong interdependency develops between the process and product stages of evaluation. Less exploration and more structure takes place. The "audit trail" provided during the process stage helps to interpret outcomes examined during the product evaluation stage.

Product Evaluation. At the product stage of evaluation, attainments are finally compared with stated program objectives to measure the degree of accomplishment obtained. Comparison of actual against intended outcomes provides recycling information needed to reexamine either program objectives, processes used to meet objectives, or both.

The Costs of Evaluation

The CIPP model of evaluation as applied to learning assistance programs is not without associated costs, and an enumeration of these costs constitutes valid criticism of the method:

1. The model is somewhat esoteric for the practitioner who may not have the background and training in evaluation; the funds available to hire a professional evaluator; or a great deal of input

into top-level decision making concerning personnel, program funding, facilities, and so forth.

2. The model implies long-range evaluation requiring a great deal of time when the practitioner is being called upon for short-range answers to pressing problems.

3. Little precedent exists for evaluation of learning assistance programs outside of the traditional methodologies (experimental design, process comparisons, congruency measures against stated objectives, and so on).

4. Chances are that the practitioner is working in a situation where underfunding and understaffing exist, institutional support (such as, population characteristics, comparison data, accurate retention data, and computer support) is difficult to obtain, and learning assistance program staff often feel like "second-class citizens" when dealing with other campus units.

Each of these costs of, or objections to, the type of evaluation suggested by the CIPP (or any similar) model is real, and no attempt will be made to minimize them. As with any decision, the alternatives must be weighed in terms of the advantageous or negative consequences, and the cost of employing any particular type of evaluation in a given situation may outweigh the possible positive outcomes.

A Practical Application in a Learning Assistance Program

An evaluation of a learning assistance program can quickly become enormous if one is tempted to begin with an overall (context) assessment of an institution, its learners, desired conditions, resources available, competing objectives and strategies, possible processes, and measurable outcomes. If such evaluation is possible, fine, but the practitioner may wish to avoid the temptation to broadly apply a decision-making model and begin instead at a level where more control (thus certainty of completion) is assured. Practice at a micro-level may lead to greater confidence in the method and later applicability to broader settings.

Assume that a study skills instructor in an already established learning assistance program relays that some of his students have requested assistance in becoming "more familiar with the campus library." There it is—an unmet need, an opportunity to apply decision-making evaluation systematically. By planning, structuring, implementing, and recycling, a micro-level test of the evaluation strategy itself may be performed. What are the decisions to be made if one employs a strategy like CIPP?

Context. The result of this stage will be objectives based upon the values and goals of the students and staff, knowledge of various ways to help students become more familiar with the library, the establishment of a baseline against which to measure "familiarity," identification of problems associated with realizing the objectives, identification of various strategies to overcome problems and meet the objectives, and an identification of audiences to receive the results of the evaluation.

Typical questions (which imply data gathering to set up the planning activities) are: What has prompted the interest in the library? Are the students freshmen with a low-level need for library resources, or are they upperclassmen who need to write extensive research papers? Are their inquiries intrinsically motivated or are they being prompted by faculty (which could lead to intrinsic motivation)? Does the library provide orientation or training sessions? Is there a library usage course on campus? Are there materials available from the library or the learning lab to design a unit of instruction? Are there catalogs of available materials? Are there similar programs elsewhere that can guide the development of a library unit? Could guest lecturing be provided? Are there learning prerequisites that should be considered? Can staff expertise be tapped?

To assist planning at this stage, "if-then" type questions may be asked: If time is spent on a library unit, then will other activities have to be sacrificed? If library personnel are utilized, then will staff be available for other responsibilities? Such questioning is considered *contingency* evaluation. Another contextual evaluation method is termed *congruency*. Intended performance is compared against actual performance. In this example, an assessment of the present level of library knowledge and usage behavior would provide congruency data as well as establish a base-line against which to measure gain.

Input Evaluation. Assuming that objectives were stated as a result of the planning (context) stage, structuring decisions will be made in the input stage. At this stage, the objectives available to meet the stated goal will be ranked in importance. Strategies will be assessed as to their human and nonhuman "costs." Strategies for time frames, curriculum designs, and feedback methods will be devised. Benefits to students, staff, and faculty might be described. People will be selected, materials will be ordered, instruments will be refined, resources will be allocated, and criteria for reporting will be further defined.

In summary, the input stage is a filter to take in the objectives, problems, and strategies and to produce an operational design. In this example, an operational design might involve a two-hour unit that includes a preassessment, a slide/tape presentation of library resources, a walk-through tour of the library, an assigned research topic, and a postassessment.

Process Evaluation. A simplistic, overriding question at this stage is "How did it go?" At this stage, defects in the pre- or postassessments may be detected. (Although field testing in the input stage would minimize such failure.) Scheduling problems with the sound/slide equipment may emerge. The walk-through tour may take too long or students may not be able to hear the presentor. The assignment may be too easy or too hard. Expected resources may not be available. Were back-up personnel needed? Were the groups too large? Was weather a problem? Did supplies run short? Were staff comfortable with the experience? Fine tuning may be needed at the process stage in order to meet the stated objectives.

Product Evaluation. Did it work? Did the students reach the stated objectives? Was the experience satisfying for them? Did transfer take place, and was there long-term retention (assuming these to be stated objectives)? This stage is both formative and summative. Feedback from the product evaluation will help determine if the objectives, strategies, and process designs were adequate. Modifications may be needed (including the possibility of not repeating the program). Phases of the program may have to be enhanced or trimmed depending upon the measured outcomes. Alternative strategies (perhaps among those previously rejected) may have to be employed. It is at the product stage that cost/benefit decisions must be made, and recycling decisions will be dependent upon the final results of all information available at that point.

Implications of Decision-Making Evaluation Methods

Purposes of Evaluation. At the spring 1981 National Association for Remedial/Developmental Studies in Postsecondary Education (NARDSPE) Conference held in Dayton, Ohio, participants at Carol Clymer Walvekar's presentation on evaluation were asked to state the purposes of evaluation. The following purposes were given: substantiate funding, demonstrate worthiness, rally support, document improvement, indicate weaknesses and strengths, diagnose student needs and the extent to which they are met, document processes, measure student performance, link to the state of the art, obtain additional funding, measure program necessity, determine proper staffing, evaluate evaluation methods, measure attitude, determine learning styles, examine the environment, examine objectives and processes, examine delivery methods, examine the organization, measure growth, and examine referral.

The reader is invited to examine the extent to which these evaluation purposes are realized by a model that focuses on decision making in a systematic way as described. While some of these purposes may be myopic, self-serving, or unresponsive, they are also realistic from a practitioner's point of view. The totality of the purposes is consistent with a broader view of evaluation.

Other Models of Evaluation. As this chapter has shown, various evaluation methodologies may be employed within the broad view of a decision-making framework. In the library example cited, professional judgment, cost-effectiveness, congruency, behavior measures, and systems approach were apparent. Clearly, an experimental design could have been employed to "prove" effectiveness, and while the evaluation was not "goal-free," it was responsive to environmental changes.

PERT, Delphi techniques, statistical analysis, computer technology, management by objectives, and other systematic techniques are certainly available as tools to aid in decision making. The emphasis here is on the decision maker, however, not on the technology employed to reach those decisions.

Conclusion

At the root of evaluation is the word *value,* and the major purpose of evaluation is to determine the value or worth of the thing (program, product) under study. Increasingly learning assistance program practitioners will be asked to evaluate the worth of their programs during the 1980s. The ability to answer value questions when they are asked, or to have a system in place that predicts when answers may be available, will become increasingly important as well. The role and scope of evaluation of learning assistance programs should be broad enough to provide practitioners with a systematic, predictable method for determining value and making value decisions.

References

Alkin, M. C., and Fitz-Gibbon, C. T. "Methods and Theories of Evaluating Programs." *Journal of Research and Development in Education,* 1975, *8* (3), 2–15.

Arnn, J., and Strickland, B. "Human Considerations in the Effectiveness of Systems Approaches." *Educational Technology,* 1975, *15,* 13–17.

Boylan, H. "Evaluating Cost-Effectiveness of Learning Center Operations." Paper presented at the American College Personnel Association Convention, Detroit, March 1978.

Braybrooke, D., and Lindblom, C. E. *A Strategy of Decision.* New York: Free Press, 1963.

Brown, R. R. "Evaluating Learning Centers." In O. T. Lenning and R. L. Nayman (Eds.), *New Directions for College Learning Assistance: New Roles for Learning Assistance,* no. 2, San Francisco: Jossey-Bass, 1980.

Campbell, D. T., and Stanley, J. C. *Experimental and Quasi-Experimental Designs for Research.* Chicago: Rand McNally, 1966.

Carss, B. W. "Systems Analysis in Education—A Statement." *Educational Product Review,* 1969, *2* (5), 43–44.

Gardner, D. E. "Five Evaluation Frameworks." *Journal of Higher Education,* 1977, *48,* 571–593.

Graham, W. J. "New Approaches to Product Management." *We Can Implement Cost-Effective Information Systems NOW.* Princeton, N.J.: EDUCOM, Inter-University Communications Council, 1976.

Haller, E. J. "Cost Analysis for Program Evaluation." In W. J. Popham (Ed.), *Evaluation in Education.* Berkeley, Calif.: McCutchan, 1974.

Heath, S. P., and Orlich, D. C. "Determining the Costs of Educational Technology:

An Exploratory Review and Analysis." *Educational Technology*, 1977, *17* (2), 26–33.

Hill, J. E. "How Schools Can Apply Systems Analysis." *Fastbacks.* No. 6. Bloomington, Ind.: Phi Delta Kappa Educational Foundation, 1972.

Land, F. "Economic Analysis of Information Systems." *We Can Implement Cost-Effective Information Systems NOW.* Princeton, N.J.: EDUCOM, Inter-University Communications Council, 1976.

Provus, M. *Discrepancy Evaluation.* Berkeley, Calif.: McCutchan, 1971.

Rosenthal, L. E. "A Model for Implementation of Computer-Based Instructional Systems." *Educational Technology*, 1976, *16*, 13–22.

Scriven, M. S. "Evaluation Perspectives and Procedures." In W. J. Popham (Ed.), *Evaluation in Education.* Berkeley, Calif.: McCutchan, 1974.

Scriven, M. S. "The Methodology of Evaluation." In R. E. Stake (Ed.), *Perspectives of Curriculum Evaluation.* No. 1. Chicago: Rand McNally, 1967.

Stake, R. E. "The Countenance of Educational Evaluation." *Teachers College Record*, 1967, *68* (7), 523–540.

Steinaker, N., and Bell, M. R. "An Evaluation Design Based on the Experiential Taxonomy." *Educational Technology*, 1976, *16*, 26–31.

Stufflebeam, D. L. "Alternative Approaches to Educational Evaluation: A Self-Study Guide for Educators." In W. J. Popham (Ed.), *Evaluation in Education.* Berkeley, Calif.: McCutchan, 1974.

Stufflebeam, and others (Eds.). *Educational Evaluation and Decision Making.* Phi Delta Kappa National Study Commission on Evaluation, Itasca, Ill.: F. E. Peacock, 1971.

Worthen, B. R., and Sanders, J. R. *Educational Evaluation: Theory and Practice.* Worthington, Ohio: Charles A. Jones, 1973.

Robert L. Moore has served as the coordinator of the Learning Resources Unit at the University of Arkansas at Fayetteville since July 1978. He previously was the associate director of the Teaching Center at the University of Florida at Gainesville.

*There are many ways to gather information to
make evaluation decisions. Carefully designed
studies can provide answers to questions and
ways to improve learning assistance programs and
judge their effectiveness.*

Using Research Designs to Evaluate Learning Assistance Programs

*Kenneth Majer
Carmel Myers*

Evaluation is an essential component of any program development. Its purpose is to provide information to make decisions. Evaluation decisions need to be made for program modification during development and to judge program success.

In the complex field of educational research and evaluation, it is sometimes easy to confuse terms like evaluation, research, and experimental design. To avoid confusion, evaluation can be thought of as the process of gathering information to make decisions. Research provides the methods for gathering valid and reliable information. Experimental design includes a number of specific techniques used in research and evaluation to determine the effect of variables of interest. Survey techniques, interviewing procedures, and library synthesis of research findings are all valid ways of gathering information to make decisions. The subject of this chapter, however, will be quasi-experimental designs and research techniques useful for evaluation (Campbell and Stanley, 1966).

Evaluation questions focus on program development and success. The design you select to answer any given question will be determined by

C. C. Walvekar (Ed.), *New Directions for College Learning Assistance: Assessment of Learning Assistance Services*, no. 5. San Francisco: Jossey-Bass, 1981.

the question and the purpose for asking it. The key is to pose the proper question and answer it accurately to be able to make a decision concerning the program. Some typical questions that can be answered using research procedures include: Does the number of contact hours in a learning assistance program significantly enhance student learning? How much time should tutees spend with tutors? Does participation in a learning assistance program, as a student or staff member, enhance performance on graduate admissions tests? How does student performance differ when self-instructional modules are compared to tutoring? Does tutoring enhance grades?

Information for Decisions

Directors of learning assistance programs need to make decisions. With limited resources, questions arise about how money should be allocated in learning assistance programs. If you can answer questions that provide information about the success of your tutorial program, that information will help you make decisions about resource allocation. For example, if students use tutors more than any other service, and student learning is enhanced by tutoring, you may have good reason to support tutoring over another service. If the benefits of a summer bridge program are most cost-effective, that may outweigh some of the advantages of some other program.

Quasi-experimental designs can be used to answer both formative and summative questions (Bloom, Hastings, and Madaus, 1971). Formative questions could relate to tutoring time and number of tutor/tutee contacts, for example. Summative decisions, such as whether to keep a particular program, can also be made by gathering reliable information using appropriate methods. Overall, the purpose of evaluation is to answer these important questions.

Evaluation questions generally provide answers for specific audiences or constituencies. Funding agencies are interested in certain types of evaluative data to help them make allocation decisions. Administrators on college and university campuses may ask questions to satisfy legislative critics or other pressure groups. Students may seek information about learning assistance programs that can help them make decisions about how to allocate their limited time among many activities. Faculty may be interested in questions about how the program supports their courses. Finally, the professional community of learning assistance program developers is interested in answers to questions about program variables that can be generalized to other learning assistance programs.

Although we encourage the use of experimental designs to gather evaluation information, we must offer one caveat: Information gained from carefully controlled experiments can be more than people want or need to know. This can cause confusion. The problem is exacerbated by the mystique of experimental design and the additional information or by-product information that can result from controlled or quasi-experimental design methods. To avoid this confusion, always answer the question, but don't provide more information than is necessary. Keep it simple. Remember your audience, and answer the question in a way that will be useful for them and that will not raise additional questions tangential to the purpose of the evaluation.

Questions for Specific Purposes

There are essentially five major reasons for asking evaluation questions: program improvement, accountability, funding, cooperation, and knowledge.

Program Improvement. Needs change, students change, new methods are introduced; for these and other reasons, learning assistance programs require continual evaluation. It is rarely the case that a program can be developed and used without making modifications based on new information or changed conditions. Because learning assistance programs are so important, program directors must have the information necessary to establish the quality of the effort. It would be an enormous waste of human effort if programs were not evaluated and there was no guarantee that the effort, time, and money were leading to desirable outcomes for students. Constant program adjustment and improvement will ensure that your learning assistance program remains a viable and useful entity. Typical program improvement questions could include: Can the same gains in student performance be achieved by replacing a labor intensive program module with a more cost-effective self-instructional unit? Which tutor training components are most effective and why? Given the new entry requirement for four years of high school English, are the skill levels of entering freshmen significantly different? If yes, what modifications are necessary for our remedial English modules? Do the latest statistics show an increased number of hispanic students entering as freshmen? Does this have implications for the number of English as a Second Language (ESL) courses we currently offer?

Accountability. In days of dwindling resources due to lower enrollments, fewer federal and state dollars, and pressures for limited funds to be spent in increasingly different ways, learning assistance programs must remain accountable. Few agencies in the eighties are going to grant money for programs without some assurance that the money is being well spent. Professional responsibility dictates that learning assistance program directors spend their resources wisely on programs that make a difference; and learning assistance center directors can be well-prepared if they ask accountability questions before someone else does. Such questions might include: What is the cost per learning assistance instructional hour for each learning assistance program? How many students utilize each program in the center? How would a 10 percent reduction in the total budget affect the program offerings and the number of students served? What would be the program impact on students with a 10 percent increase in funding? What percentage of the center's total budget is spent on direct service delivery, administration, supplies and related expenses, overhead, and so forth?

Funding. Whether you seek federal, state, or local campus resources, arguments need to be made for appropriations. Evaluation data provide the best way to argue for funding. Often these data do not need to be highly technical and based on complicated research designs. They can simply be descriptive, including percentages and frequency data that show usage, appropriate clientele for which you were funded (ethnicity, grade point average or performance scores), and number of contacts by program. Questions to ask could include: How many students use the program? What proportion of underrepresented minority students use your program? Which programs are used most frequently? What is the grade point average of the students using your programs?

Cooperation. No program exists in a vacuum. The political nature and administrative structure of your campus will surely affect your program. The degree of cooperation that you can acquire from various people on your campus could influence program success. For example, if your learning assistance program includes remedial components for specific courses, faculty cooperation becomes very important. Questions that can be asked to enhance this type of cooperation could include the following: Does the learning assistance program writing adjunct improve grades of student papers in political science? Can the learning assistance program mathematics diagnostic test provide useful information to the math department for proper assignment of specific students to specific courses? What effect do the remedial groups in chemistry have on students who perform poorly on the first midterm exam? Do learning assistance program calculus tutors provide adequate help to students having difficulty in Calculus 101?

Knowledge. Finally, more generic questions can be asked that add to the literature of the field. Sharing information from program to program can help learning assistance program directors make decisions about the kinds of programs they wish to implement or components of programs they may wish to incorporate. Answering these questions requires careful control of experimental variables and clear descriptions of research methods to be able to generalize the conclusions to other campus settings. Answers to the following types of questions could provide useful information to other learning assistance program directors: Which components of a tutor training course are most effective when training tutors? What is the relationship between ethnicity of tutors and minority use of the tutoring program? Can deficits in entry-level skills at college be eliminated with participation in the learning assistance program? After a full year of regular campus participation, how do the grades of participants in a summer bridge program compare to those of nonparticipants? What effect does regular attendance at tutoring appointments have on student performance?

In the following sections, we have categorized evaluation questions by type of information required. These are realistic examples of questions that have been asked by the research staff of the learning assistance program at the Office of Academic Support and Instructional Services (OASIS) of the University of California at San Diego (UCSD). Each of the examples illustrates designs to answer a question of the types we have categorized: questions of effectiveness or benefit, about relationship, concerning follow-up and long-term effectiveness, and about specific program variables. Each sample question is clarified, the method for answering the question is described, selected results are given, and answers to the questions plus the limitations of the answers are presented.

Questions of Effectiveness or Benefit

Does tutoring have a long-term effect?

The Question. How does the freshman grade point average (GPA) of Educational Opportunity Program (EOP) students who received tutoring compare to EOP students who did not receive tutoring? This question was investigated by Hedges and Majer (1976b) to determine the effectiveness of the OASIS tutorial program with this special group.

Method. Subjects for this four-year study comprised groups of EOP freshmen who entered UCSD during fall quarter, 1971, 1972, and 1973. The experimental groups consisted of students who received tutoring their freshman year. During the 1971–72 academic year, tutees were referred by faculty members while during 1972–73 and 1973–74 academic years, all EOP freshmen were invited to seek tutorial assistance. For each experimental group, a control group was randomly selected from EOP freshmen who entered in the same year but did not receive tutoring.

Three analyses were performed. First, the cumulative freshman GPAs of the three experimental and control groups were compared in separate analyses with a one-way analysis of covariance design. High school GPA, SAT mathematics score, and SAT verbal score, were used as covariates to compensate for the initial differences in ability between the experimental and control groups. The groups were tracked through their sophomore year, during which time none of the students were tutored.

The freshman year and sophomore year overall grade point averages were computed for students in each of the groups who persisted through their sophomore year. For each of the three samples, the data were analyzed by a two-by-two repeated analysis of variance to determine whether there was an interaction between tutoring/nontutoring treatment and the year in which GPA was measured.

Finally, the retention rate during the sophomore year was computed for each group. For each of the three samples in the study, a two-by-two contingency table was constructed, indicating the number of students who remained in school versus the number of students who dropped out. A chi-square was computed for each contingency table to test the hypothesis that the retention rate for the experimental and control groups was not significantly different.

Selected Results. One of the comparisons in this study used an analysis of variance to compare the freshman GPA and sophomore GPA of the freshmen who were tutored or untutored during the 1971–72 academic year. Only students who persisted through their sophomore year were included in the analysis. While the main effects of the tutoring and class levels were not statistically significant, the interaction effect in this analysis was significant, $F(1,106) = 4.119$, $p \leq .05$. This interaction indicates that the grades of students who were tutored as freshmen tended to increase between the freshman and sophomore years relative to the grades of the untutored group.

Answers and Limitations. The results of this study provide evidence of the positive impact of the tutorial program on students' grade point averages. In each of the three replications of the study, tutored EOP freshmen achieved significantly higher adjusted GPAs than the control group of untutored EOP freshmen. These differences are not only statistically significant, but are educationally significant as well.

The results of this study also support the notion that EOP students who are tutored as freshmen are likely to increase their grade point averages as sophomores. This result occurred in two of the three replications, indicating that tutored students tended to increase their GPAs (relative to untutored students) in their sophomore year. These results underscore the fact that tutoring not only produced higher student achievement but tutees retained their level of achievement more than untutored students did, and actually increased their GPAs after tutoring had ceased.

The significance of the long-term effect of tutoring on tutees is further substantiated by the results indicating that tutees had significantly lower sophomore year attrition than untutored students in two of the three replications. Thus, not only do the former tutees' grades increase with respect to nontutees, but the former tutees also exhibit lower attrition.

One of the most serious limiting factors in a study such as this is self-selection. In the UCSD tutoring program, students are not required to have tutoring. Students who avail themselves of this opportunity do seem to be helped by it. However, those students may be more highly motivated anyway. It is impossible to determine whether the achievement gains would have been found with these specific students if they had not taken advantage of the tutoring opportunity.

Questions About Relationship

What is the relationship of female and minority representation in college majors as a function of mathematics requirements?

The Question. Black female, Chicano female, Asian female, and total female enrollment representations as well as total black, total Chicano, and total Asian enrollment representations were determined for undergraduate major areas at seven University of California campuses (Hedges and Majer, 1976a). The number of mathematics courses required for each major was also determined from the catalog for each campus. The question concerned the correlation between the number of math courses required for majors and the number of females and minority students by major.

Method. The percentage of women in each major was computed for each campus. The number of mathematics courses required for graduation in each major was also computed for each campus. This was done by adding the number of high school mathematics courses plus the number of university-level mathematics courses required. The data for all campuses were combined and a Pearson product-movement correlation between the representation of women in majors and the number of math courses required for those majors was then computed.

In addition, the percentage of students who identified themselves as blacks, Chicanos, and Asians, respectively, were computed for each major at each campus. Data were combined from all campuses for each group, and the correlation between representation in majors and the number of math courses required for the majors was computed.

Finally, the representation of black females, Asian females, and Chicano females, respectively, was computed for each major. Again, data from all campuses were pooled and correlations between representation in majors and the number of math courses required for the majors were computed.

Selected Results. The results of the correlational analysis and significance tests were consistent. Except for Asians, there was a significant negative relationship between representation in major fields and number of mathematics courses required in that major. (All women $r = -.567$; black women $r = -2.04$; Chicano women $r = -2.21$; Asian women $r = -.048$; all blacks $r = -.112$; all Chicanos $r = -.116$; all Asians $r = +.114$.)

Answers and Limitations. This study seems to confirm that an underlying variable in the distribution of women students among disciplines is the mathematics requirement for that discipline. Although previous studies have noted that comparatively few women are enrolled in the physical sciences, for example, they have not demonstrated mathematics requirements as a factor.

Minority representation in the sciences is lower than in most other areas of study. Many of the same arguments that have been voiced about this low minority participation in the sciences have been voiced for women. This study supports the notion that an underlying factor in the differential minority representation among various major fields of study is the amount of mathematics coursework required for those majors. There was a significant positive correlation between the number of mathematics courses required and Asian representation in the major. This trend would be expected from data on representation in the sciences, where Asians are overrepresented in proportion to their overall enrollment.

The most significant limitation of correlational analyses that describe relationships is the lack of ability to draw causal inferences. While the low representation of women and minorities in a given discipline is not necessarily caused by lower mathematical achievement, there is a relationship between these two variables.

Questions About Follow-Up and Long-Term Effectiveness

What is the long-term effect of a summer bridge program for Educational Opportunity Program Students?

The Question. One of the learning assistance programs at UCSD is a summer bridge program designed to provide experiences for underprepared students before they enter the regular freshman year. Follow-up studies were conducted on the 1978 UCSD summer bridge program after one full year and two full years of university work (Myers and Drevlow, 1979; Myers and Drevlow, 1980). These reports follow up the 1978 summer bridge students and five comparison groups, including alternates, nonrespondents, noninvited EOP students, non-EOP students, and summer bridge dropouts. Comparisons are made for the use of OASIS services, academic standing, current and cumulative grades, and units taken. Persistence rates of students over time are compared.

Method. The subjects were the original 90 EOP students invited to attend summer bridge and 90 randomly selected first-quarter freshmen of whom 45 were EOP and 45 were non-EOP. For the purpose of analysis, the 180 students were divided into six groups. *Participants,* or bridge students, were those students who attended the summer bridge program ($n=28$). *Alternates* were those students who wanted to attend summer bridge but could not because of enrollment restrictions (*n*=15). *Nonrespondents* were those students who did not respond to the invitation to attend summer bridge (*n*=45). *Noninvited EOP* were randomly selected EOP freshmen not invited to attend summer bridge (*n*=45). *Non-EOP* were randomly selected EOP freshmen (*n*=45). *Bridge dropouts* were those students who dropped out of the summer bridge program (*n*=2) prior to having completed the activities. (One student did not attend at all and one left after one week.)

Comparisons of these groups were made at the end of spring quarter, using data from the entire 1979–80 academic year. Initial differences in SAT scores and evaluated high school grade point averages (EHSGPA) were held constant when testing for group differences in grade point averages and units taken.

Selected Results. Of the entire 180 students in the sample, 112 completed their second year at UCSD for an overall persistence rate of 62 percent. Persistance rates by group were as follows: participants = 82 percent; alternates = 67 percent; nonrespondents = 31 percent; noninvited EOP = 71 percent; non-EOP = 69 percent; and bridge dropouts = 50 percent.

It is clear that bridge participants had the highest persistence rate at the end of spring quarter, and nonrespondents had the lowest rate. A chi-square was performed to test for independence between persistence rates and group category. A significant chi-square, $\chi^2 = 25.62$, $p \leqslant .001$ indicated that group membership was related to persistence.

Of the orginial 180 students, 85 were retained to the beginning of fall quarter 1980 for an overall retention rate of 47.2 percent after two years. Bridge participants had the highest retention rate, which was 64.3 percent. Non-EOP and noninvited EOP had retention rates of 53.3 percent and 55.6 percent, respectively. Nonrespondents had the lowest rate, 22.2 percent, and alternates had a 46.7 percent retention rate.

Two comparisons are particularly interesting. First, bridge participants exceeded the retention rate of alternates by 17.6 percent. In this comparison, self-selection and motivational variables are best controlled. Second, when participants are excluded from the computation of a total retention rate for the other three EOP groups (alternates, nonrespondents, and noninvited EOP), the EOP retention rate is 40 percent compared with 64.3 percent for bridge participants. Finally, retention by EOP status is important. Non-EOP students did not have significantly higher retention rates than EOP students (bridge participants and other EOP combined).

Answers and Limitations. Compared with other groups, bridge participants had the highest persistence rate at the end of spring quarter 1980. Thus, bridge participants were more likely to complete their second academic year than any of the other groups. Participants' persistence was well over twice that of students who did not respond to the original summer bridge invitation. There may be motivational relationships between wanting to attend summer bridge and completing two years of school, which may explain the persistence differences. However, those who were presumably as motivated to attend bridge as were participants (but could not because of enrollment restrictions) persisted at a lower rate than did participants. It would appear that this 15 percent difference reasonably could be attributed to the summer bridge program.

Thus, the main objective of the summer bridge program, which is to increase the retention of EOP students, was achieved. After two years, summer bridge participants have been retained at a rate of eleven percentage points higher than regularly admitted traditional students and twenty-four percentage points higher than comparison EOP groups.

Questions About Specific Program Variables

What is the effect of regular attendance at tutoring appointments on student performance?

The Question. Cancelled or failed attendance at appointments was a behavior of concern to OASIS staff because it appeared that irregularity in attendance could have an affect on achievement and scheduling. These issues were investigated by Drevlow and Myers (1979).

Method. To test the hypotheses and to examine other possible differences among the students, the following information was collected for analysis: SAT scores, EHSGPAs, sex, EOP status, class, college, academic standing, course being tutored, grade in tutored course (if completed), fall quarter units, fall quarter GPA, and cumulative GPA.

The subjects were 88 of the 102 students who had regular appointments. The subjects were divided into four categories: *no shows* were those who simply did not keep their appointments ($n=11$). *Less than 50 percent* were those who came in to less than half of their appointments ($n=17$). *50 percent or more* were those who came in for at least half of their appointments ($n=52$). *Cancelled* were those who cancelled their appointments and did not make new ones ($n=11$).

Selected Results. Sixty-four percent of the subjects were female. A chi-square was performed to see if either sex had a tendency to be disproportionately represented in any of the comparison groups, but the result was not significant ($\chi^2 = 4.813$; ns).

Average SAT scores were also examined by category. An analysis of variance revealed no significant difference among the groups in SAT quantitative or verbal scores. In addition, EOP students were more likely to be no shows than expected, and less likely than expected to attend 50 percent or more of the sessions.

A total of 35 students (38 percent) were on probation or subject to dismissal at the end of fall quarter 1978. With students on probation and subject to dismissal combined, a chi-square was performed to test for independence between group category and academic standing. The resulting statistic was not significant ($\chi^2 = 1.111$; ns), indicating no tendency for any one category to be more likely to be in good or poor standing.

Finally, average fall grade point average, fall quarter units, and cumulative GPA by category were compared using an analysis of covariance with SAT scores and EHSGPA covariates. No significant differences in any of these variables were found among the groups.

Answers and Limitations. There do not appear to be any clear differences among tutees who keep, cancel, or do not keep their standing appointments. Their entering characteristics are the same and their grades, GPAs, and units are independent of their category status. Thus, the hypotheses posited were not confirmed. Instead, the following results were obtained: (1) students who cancelled or failed to attend their appointments were as likely to complete their tutored courses as those who kept their appointments; (2) students who regularly attended their appointments did not receive higher grades in their tutored courses compared with other students; and (3) there were no significant initial differences among the groups in sex, SAT scores, or EHSGPAs, although there were differences among the group in EOP status, with regard to regular attendance.

Clearly, these are rather specific results based upon specific program variables. The limitations, of course, are that they cannot necessarily be generalized to other programs or to other campuses. However, the practical implications for this evaluation study are important for program adjustments for more efficient operation of the tutorial program.

Carefully controlled investigations of specific program variables can often lead to lengthy documentation to explain the nature of the appropriate controls and methodology. An excellent application of a complex experimental design applied to a practical setting can be found in *OASIS Research Report* #7 (Myers, 1978), which reports the effect of self-monitoring and a combination of self-monitoring, self-reinforcement, and self-punishment of study time on test performance. Due to space limitation here, this study is not reported. However, it is available upon request.

Conclusion

Evaluation activities are an integral part of program development. Data for evaluation are gathered for making decisions about program modifications or program effectiveness. While there are many methods for collecting data to make evaluation decisions, we have focused on some practical questions that can be answered by applying experimental or quasi-experimental techniques.

The most important message we are trying to convey is that evaluation techniques, including quasi-experimental designs, are to be applied as

62

tools to answer practical questions that arise about learning assistance programs. Questions of program efficacy can be asked in ways that help make comparisons, examine relationships, analyze effectiveness and benefits of program activities, examine follow-up and long-term effects, and analyze specific program variables for their impact. The particular technique used is a function of the specific evaluation questions. Answering questions to provide information to program directors is the essence of practical evaluation for learning assistance program developers.

References

Bloom, B. S., Hastings, J. G., and Madaus, G. F. *Handbook on Formative and Summative Evaluation of Student Learning.* New York: McGraw-Hill, 1971.

Campbell, D. T., and Stanley J. C. *Experimental and Quasi-Experimental Designs for Research.* Chicago: Rand McNally, 1966.

Drevlow, S., and Myers C. A. *OASIS Research Report #9: The Effect of Regular Attendance at Tutoring Appointments on Students Performance.* La Jolla: Office of Academic Support and Instructional Services, University of California, San Diego, 1979.

Hedges, L. V., and Majer, K. *OASIS Research Report #4: An Attempt to Improve Prediction of College Success of Minority Students by Adjusting for High School Characteristics.* La Jolla: Office of Academic Support and Instructional Services, University of California, San Diego, 1976a.

Hedges, L. V., and Majer, K. *OASIS Research Report #5: A Longitudinal Comparative Study of a Process-Oriented Tutorial Program.* La Jolla: Office of Academic Support and Instructional Services, University of California, San Diego, 1976b.

Myers, C. A. *OASIS Research Report #7: Effects of Self-Monitoring, Self-Reinforcement, and Self-Punishment of Study Time on Test Performance.* La Jolla: Office of Academic Support and Instructional Services, University of California, San Diego, 1978.

Myers, C. A., and Drevlow, S. *OASIS Research Report #8: Summer Bridge Program, Fall Quarter, 1978, Follow-Up.* La Jolla: Office of Academic Support and Instructional Services, University of California, San Diego, 1979.

Myers, C. A., and Drevlow, S. *OASIS Research Report #15: The 1978 Summer Bridge Program: Second Year Follow-Up.* La Jolla: Office of Academic Support and Instructional Services, University of California, San Diego, 1980.

Kenneth Majer is the director of the Office of Academic Support and Instructional Services at the University of California, San Diego. He is currently on leave from UCSD to develop a California State Department of Education program to establish entry-level college competencies and a federally sponsored international academic support program in southern Africa.

Carmel Myers is acting director, Office of Academic Support and Instructional Services at the University of California, San Diego. She received her Ph.D. in educational psychology from Michigan State University and has worked in learning centers and with data systems for six years. In 1976 she developed the OASIS data base, which provides information on over 3,000 students served in UCSD's learning assistance center.

*Introducing computers into learning assistance
program evaluations requires thorough consideration
of data needs and careful planning that involves all
members of the staff.*

Using Computers
in Evaluation

Carmel Myers
Kenneth Majer

The use of computers in learning assistance programs has increased as the
demand for information about programs has grown. No longer are federal,
state, or local funding sources content with narrative statements about
program offerings and anecdotal accounts of student success. Numbers are
a big part of reports, and computers do numbers well.

A quick glance at the reports required by the U.S. Department of
Education for learning assistance programs gives a good example of data
requirements for evaluation. Information is required about the total
number of students served and the number of students by various categories, such as ethnicity, sex, and veteran status. Further, requests are made of
project directors to provide the amount and type of service students have
received (tutoring, peer counseling, study skills, and so forth). Finally,
information is also required about what happens to students after the
program has ended. How many are continuing in the program? How many
are continuing in school? How many have transferred, flunked out,
dropped out, graduated? Basically, agencies want to know what the
students are like, what services they have received, and what happened to
them after service. And they want this information in numbers.

C. C. Walvekar (Ed.), *New Directions for College Learning Assistance: Assessment
of Learning Assistance Services,* no. 5. San Francisco: Jossey-Bass, 1981.

Back at the state and campus level, similar questions are asked. However, more precise information is often required about students' academic performance, numbers of credits completed, choice of major, and so forth. Specific comparisons may also be requested, such as a comparison between high school and postsecondary performance or a comparison between groups that have received learning assistance and groups that have not. Requests are also made to compare students by sex, major, ethnicity, college, parents' occupation, parents' income, and more. Sometimes requests are made for comparisons of several of these variables at once. For example, what were the grades and credits completed by sex within each major? Or what is the retention rate of students by ethnicity and income level?

It should be obvious that just keeping track of all of this information becomes very time-consuming. If a learning assistance program is serving very many students at all, collecting such data and reporting them is even more demanding. This is where computers can help.

Let's begin by asking five questions about our data needs: What do we want to know? Where can we get it? When can we get it? How can we collect it so it is minimally intrusive? and Why do we need to know it? The answers to these questions will give us a foundation of information about our programs called a data base. For clarity, we will consider each question separately, but in practice we are most likely to consider several questions simultaneously.

Five Questions on the Way to a Data Base

What Do We Need to Know? This is the first question we need to ask. The answer will generally result in a list that includes student's name, identification number, address, telephone number, birthdate, sex, ethnicity, and the date. The list may also include the academic quarter or semester, whether the student is a veteran, physically disabled, or a transfer student. What is the student's class level, major, college? Is English the first language? If not, what is? Is the student an Educational Opportunity Program (EOP) student? Is the student on financial aid? What were the student's SAT or ACT scores? What was the past high school or college grade point average (GPA)? What is the student's cumulative and current GPA? Is he or she on probation? What services were received? How many contacts did the student have? In addition, we may have to assign students codes that show their eligibility to receive services so that we can report to our funding services.

The first step, then, is to make a long list of what we want to know, based on a careful review of required reports; analysis of the program's information needs; and consultation with learning assistance staff and other groups of faculty, students, and staff.

Where Can We Get It? Now that we know what we want, consider where we can obtain the information. Next to each item, we should list one to three sources. For example, a student's name could be obtained from an application, from an intake form, or from a referral. However, to ensure accuracy, we probably want to get GPA and units from an official record. We can obtain SAT scores from the application, high school transcript, or the Educational Testing Service. Our basic sources of information are these: the application, the student, our own records (number of units, type of service), and school records (transcripts and other printouts or reports).

When Can We Get It? After our column of whats and wheres, we need to add a third column of whens. Basically, questions about when can be answered by grouping data sources into "before service," "at the onset of service," "during service," or "after service." Sometimes a source will be available to us, but not in time for us to consult the source, handcount or code the data, keypunch it, and produce a report. Then, we have to turn to another source. Or we may have to seek a change in the report due date.

It is important to use a calendar to look at the academic year as well as our what, when, and where columns. We need to note report due dates and the content required. We need to examine our program activities and the type of information we need at each stage. We must put on our calendars the dates (when) that information (what) is available. We also must now consider the time it takes to code and keypunch data, estimate programming and computer time, and project time to write and produce a report.

Thus, we'll be able to see potential problems and deal with them in advance. We are much more credible if we say in October, "Ah, well, I have discovered that your report requests information on student GPA in early January, and our registrar doesn't even have fall semester data until the third week of January. It will take me at least two weeks to code it, keypunch it, and write a report for you. That means February 15 is a realistic due date." If, instead, we wait until January to say, "Well, my report is late because of the Registrar's Office," it looks like an excuse. If we anticipate such problems and explain in advance why the report must be prepared later, we will gain points for good management.

Finally, preplanning is necessary to be able to allow the computer, our secretary, or ourselves to be "down" or out of commission unexpectedly for a few hours or days and still meet deadlines. Yes, there will be emergencies, but they should be unusual. Our dependence on a whole other system requires that we must give ourselves leeway and be thorough in our planning.

How Can We Collect It so It Is Minimally Intrusive? So far, we do not need technical knowledge or expertise. We are asking and answering questions that are managerial and require the program director's involvement and leadership. We must consult other offices (computer services and keypunch), but we do that all the time (academic advisors, financial aid). Nothing new is really required.

When we reach the how question, assuming for the moment that we will use computers, we need to consult someone who is technically skilled. But we must remember that such expertise does not extend to managing a learning assistance center. Expert advice is essential and will refine our thinking. We will have to compromise on issues to accommodate the expert's advice, but learning center directors must maintain the decision-making role. Remember, we do not have secretaries write reports; we ask them to type them. Neither do our accountants make budget decisions just because they keep the books. Similarly, computer programmers and consultants give us advice and help; but final decisions are our responsibility.

Now we will consider how to collect our data so it is minimally intrusive. We have three options. First, we can use forms that are self-carboning, with the top copy sent directly to keypunch and the bottom copy kept at the program office. This type of form may often be used as an "intake form" at the onset of service. It usually contains basic information the student can provide accurately.

Second, we can use single-page forms, completed by the student or staff member, that include information about the student during service. (What services were received and how much contact was there?) These forms may be called "counselor reports" or "student service reports." They may include anecdotal information that is useful to staff who deliver service and other information we need that is more quantitative.

In order to be useful in our data base, the information from the second type of form must usually be transferred to a coding form, our third option. Computer centers have these standard, eighty-column forms that correspond to eighty-column cards, the basic diet of a computer. Much of the information in our data base will be coded on such forms because it will not be possible to obtain it in a form that is readily keypunched, or already on a computer file to which we have timely access. For example, information obtained before service (SAT scores, GPAs), during service (amount and type of services), and after service (academic performance, units completed) will generally be entered on a coding form. (There are other methods for those who have state-of-the-art equipment. The same principles apply, but cards are not required, as data are entered directly onto tape or disk files.)

So, the "how can we collect it" question is answered by designing an intake form that is quick and easy for students to complete. This starts the student's record in our program and in the computer. Then, we update that record with information about the student form before, during, and after service, using the intake form and our anecdotal records and other forms, which are transferred to coding forms to be keypunched.

At this point, someone with some technical knowledge about computers and computer files should be consulted to help design the layout of information in the computer file (also called a tape layout), the coding form, and the intake form. Most often the information we want to have can be included in two or three eighty-column cards, which make a 160- to 240-character record for each student. If information is kept for several terms or the entire period of enrollment, the record will grow longer just like a paper file would get thicker. We should, though, try to keep our system fairly simple and understandable. Many times a student worker majoring in computer science or a related field, can provide this technical assistance. If not, computer center consultants are generally available.

To be effective, the learning assistance program manager or director must understand the data base and system to be implemented. This understanding is best achieved by an intimate involvement with the design of the computer tape layout, coding forms, and all other forms, including the development of procedures for data gathering. If we let the design stage get out of control, we may not end up with a system that is "minimally intrusive." If students and staff find themselves inordinately involved in filling out forms or completing progress reports when they should be giving or receiving service, we may lose cooperation. Our leadership is a must to keep the system realistic and manageable.

Why do we need to know it? One reason—we have to. The days are over when our programs existed in some unexamined corner of the campus. Money is tight, accountability is fashionable, and concern is increasing about students' basic skills. Learning assistance programs are receiving more attention as faculty and staff look around for someone to help with these declining skill levels. Using data to demonstrate effectiveness is essential. Another reason—we should. We're in this business to make a difference. How do we know we have made a difference if we don't keep track of our students, the service they receive, and the results that occur?

Effectiveness is a complicated issue, but, again, we are more credible if we say with authority, "We served 1,800 students last semester, of whom 35 percent were minority students, 48 percent were women, and 22 percent were on probation. The students we served had higher GPAs two quarters after service when compared with other students." Then, we can be taken seriously if we add, "However, it is inappropriate to compare the grades of the students we tutored in math with the students we didn't tutor, because the students we did tutor had lower SAT math scores to begin with." It is clear, then, that we do know what our program results are, and we can discuss the results intelligently.

We must be able to address these issues because sooner or later they are going to come up. As staff of learning assistance programs, in a time of competition for dollars, we need to be able to explain why we should continue to receive funds for drop-in writing assistance when the Literature Department claims, for example, it could solve the basic writing problem with another FTE. If we can't provide clear data showing success, then maybe the Literature Department should have a chance!

Minority programs, some say, are always being scrutinized, analyzed, and required to defend themselves. Most learning assistance programs are for all students, but the major funding sources requiring reports are often those which fund special additional services for ethnic minorities, low-income students, and similar special groups. Thus, data are typically collected on all students in the learning assistance program, but the reason systems may have been set up is to account for such special funds. We must accept that if we are going to get special money, we are going to have to play by special rules.

Further, why is a very important question to discuss with staff in advance of and during the development of a data collection system. Such discussion will allow concerns to be aired, frustrations to be shared, and fears of failure to be addressed. Resistance by staff can seriously undermine the quality of information collected and, most importantly, the entire program. Staff must feel their concerns are heard. Only then will a system be designed that meets their needs and allows them to cooperate fully.

To Compute or Not Compute—That Is the Question

Returning to the development of our data collection system, we must consider whether we will do all of this planning and keep a hand-count system or take the step and computerize. That decision will be different from one campus to another, but certain factors are common to the decision. First, do we serve very many students? If we serve 100 to 200 students, it's probably not necessary to computerize, though there's no harm. It won't cost that much less or more, and may make life a little easier once the system is up and running. If we have more than a few hundred students and more than one funding source requiring information, we will probably benefit a good deal from computerizing.

Two Rules for Computerizing. A most important question at this point is: "Compute what?" Rule 1 is this: *If the data will be used only once and never needed again, let's not put it in our computer data base.* For example, forty-seven students take a study skills class and complete an evaluation of the course. You intend to use the evaluation to refine the course for the next term and that's it. Don't bother adding to each student record whether he or she "agrees strongly," "agrees," "disagrees," or "disagrees strongly" with each of sixteen questions you ask. You are only interested in general information about the class. Have a student tally the responses for you, give you the average response per question, and be done with it.

Conversely, if the data are likely to be used repeatedly, or are a necessary part of historical records you keep on your students, then computerize. Most of the information we have discussed so far is reasonable to computerize. Student satisfaction ratings are not.

Rule 2: Keep the System as Simple as Possible. For example, record the high school GPA, but don't let anyone convince you to pick up individual course grades. If two staff members want to know the relationship between high school physics performance, SAT math scores, and college science achievement, acknowledge the potential worth of this idea. Then help them or send them to someone to help them design a small research study. They can computerize their data, but not as a part of your data base. Similarly, if you want to do such a study, do it as a research project separately from the data base.

Reviewing the What, Where, When. Take some time, now to look again at your lists of what, where, when. Then, see how much data can be obtained on forms to go directly to keypunch. Find out what can be obtained by transferring information from another tape file (the Registrar's Office) to your tape file. Identify what must be coded and entered into your file because it's not available, or not available in a timely fashion from another computer file. Meet with the keypunch supervisors and learn how much lead time they need. Learn what resources (student staff, computer center consultant, systems office) are available to use for running programs. You'll seldom need to have new programs written. Packages like the *Statistical Package for the Social Sciences* (SPSS) will be able to do most of what you need done. See how much it will cost to keep your data in the computer and how much your programs are likely to cost. Find out where computer terminals are located and whether you could afford to buy one or share one with another office.

Advantages and Disadvantages. Consider the advantages and disadvantages. There are disadvantages to computers. First of all, they do not save time. Strike that myth from the record. It is true that they compute quickly, but several people must first collaborate to get all those numbers into the computer. That takes time.

Second, they do not eliminate tedium. Students must fill out forms that can go directly to keypunch centers. Clerks must code data on coding forms. Keypunchers must produce cards with all of this information from students and clerks. Program staff must review printouts of data and correct errors (after grumbling that they should be serving students). Programmers must write programs or run packaged ones to obtain the counts for reports. Then, data must be typed from computer printouts into tables. Program managers must review these tables, make interpretations, analyze information, and write narratives.

Third, the data from your data base will be quantitative. That is a limitation of computers. Our reports, then, will tend to become more numerical and less anecdotal. We must guard against the danger that we will only consider valid and interesting information that is numerical. We must be sure our reports include description, analysis, anecdotes, and discussion.

Fourth, all of these reports get read by someone, and in many cases this generates a new set of questions, more complex than the first. "Of course, since you have it all on computer, it wouldn't be that hard to get me a report on the effect of . . . ," says the student review committee, your staff, the faculty. Repeat: Computers do not save time.

But computers do have advantages. First, if you are serving more than a few hundred students, the various computations can be extremely time-consuming. We've already noted that computational time can be saved, but in this case, a penny saved is a penny spent. Someone had to code and keypunch all those data. So, the main advantage is not time saved in computation. The main advantage is that we have the data in a reusable form that allows us to ask and answer better questions. Answering more and better questions can be an advantage if it allows us to improve our programs and better serve our students.

Second, computers are here to stay, and we as program managers must come to understand and use this tool the same way we incorporated videotape training for our peer counselors, calculators for administrative assistants, and electric typewriters or word processors for our secretaries. This means we must upgrade our managerial skills by properly incorporating computers into our programs. This requires our intimate involvement and careful review of our operations.

Thus, a third advantage, which could be the most important of all, is that working with computers requires us to be more organized, systematic, and thorough.

Computers won't save time overall, and they will cost money. Initially, there are costs for design, forms, and trial runs. At the beginning, your time involvement is great and this requires a financial commitment. So, unless there are some very good reasons—complexity of report demands, large numbers of students, demands for evidence of long-term effectiveness—think twice, maybe three times, before you computerize. But, if you do, remember to stay involved and keep it simple. The advantages will then outweigh the disadvantages.

Data Collection and Evaluation

Up until now we have been discussing data collection, not evaluation. There is a cartoon from *The New Yorker* that shows an emcee standing to the left of a stage with six numbers dressed up as humans. The emcee says "Tonight, we're going to let statistics speak for themselves." To some of us, this is a very funny cartoon because statistics don't ever speak for themselves. We must carefully select the information that goes in, and it must be analyzed when it comes out. And that is an extremely important point.

Collecting data and producing tables are only two steps in the evaluation process that begins, once again, with the program director. The program director, together with learning assistance center staff have goals and objectives for the programs. These goals and objectives may be implicit in the activities that are funded or explicitly listed in program statements. In either case, they are present. Evaluation occurs when an analysis is made of goals and objectives in light of data collected. Further, the data that are quantifiable, and therefore computerized, may be only part of the analysis that occurs when objectives are matched against outcome measures. An excellent discussion of overall evaluation issues is contained in Robert R. Brown's article "Evaluating Learning Centers" (1980) and other chapters in this book. This discussion of the introduction of computers into learning assistance center evaluation efforts, however, has been limited to procedures for developing a system to gather and computerize information. It is, as you know, a complicated process, but such procedures are only one step toward evaluation.

Conclusion

This step toward evaluation begins with consideration of five important questions that build the foundation of our data base. Decisions about whether or not to computerize the data come next, and advantages and disadvantages must be carefully weighed. In addition, distinctions must be made between our data base information and research projects that require more detail; care must be taken to remember that data collection is not the same as evaluation; and the director of the learning assistance center must remain the leader of an effort that requires collaboration with center staff, other offices, and technicians. However, if careful analysis precedes technical development, and if responsibility for the data remains in the center, it is apparent that systematizing data collection and computerizing information can be very valuable for learning assistance centers.

Reference

Brown, R. R. "Evaluating Learning Centers." In O. T. Lenning and R. L. Nayman (Eds.), *New Directions for College Learning Assistance: New Roles for Learning Assistance*, no. 2. San Francisco: Jossey-Bass, 1980.

*Carmel Myers is acting director, Office of Academic Support
and Instructional Services at the University of California, San
Diego. She received her Ph.D. in educational psychology from
Michigan State University and has worked in learning centers
and with data systems for six years. In 1976 she developed the
OASIS data base, which provides information on over 3,000
students served in UCSD's learning assistance center.*

*Kenneth Majer is the director of the Office of Academic
Support and Instructional Services at the University of
California at San Diego. He is currently on leave from UCSD
to develop a California State Department of Education
program to establish entry level college competencies and a
federally sponsored international academic support program
in southern Africa.*

Vast differences in learning assistance programs,
learning styles, and learners make evaluation of
learning a very complex task.

Evaluating Learning: The Buck Stops Here

Carol Clymer Walvekar

School had been in session only one week of the fall term when I received a panicked call from a colleague: "I have a student here who's going to need some help. He's having some trouble with reading. Can you see him right away?"

I met with the student that day and quickly learned that "trouble" was somewhat understated. "Crisis" was more accurate. The student was unusually open and calm about his lack of skill in reading, and indicated that he had been tested around the sixth-grade level—several times. I did not need to give him another standardized reading test to confirm his perceptions. I opened a book, the lowest level I could find, and asked him to read. His performance was astounding. He easily read the word "scholarship," but he pondered over "burn" for minutes, and I soon pronounced it for him. We worked together in several more sessions and I learned more about his capabilities. My initial diagnosis was that he had a minimum amount of skills and a maximum amount of motivation. His potential was somewhere in between. He was about to pursue a college career with high hopes but realistic fears. I was there to give him all the help I could.

Most of us in learning assistance programs could tell similar anecdotes in reading as well as writing, speaking, and mathematics. We wonder what some students have been doing for twelve years of public education

C. C. Walvekar (Ed.), *New Directions for College Learning Assistance: Assessment of Learning Assistance Services*, no. 5. San Francisco: Jossey-Bass, 1981.

and what their teachers have been doing as well. As much as possible, we try not to condemn or blame either of the parties because we know that things are tough, and there are many problems in our school system and society in general. Most of all, we try not to pass the buck when the student walks in our door, and we start by determining, as specifically as possible, where the student is and where the student needs to, wants to, and can realistically be.

We do not always use standardized tests to determine these things; sometimes we just talk with the learner and gain far more information than any test could possibly give. Fortunately, not all of the students with whom we work are lacking in basic skills. Many are average or good students who want to be better students, or who want "to learn more in less time with greater ease and confidence" (Christ, 1971, p. 33). But all of them have different needs, abilities, backgrounds, and habits and the necessity to acknowledge these differences is crucial when providing an effective learning assistance service.

Patricia Heard (1976, pp. 6–7) recognized that "learning centers must, of necessity, be in accord with the philosophies, values, and objectives of the individuals they serve. There can never be only one exact model for learning centers; institutions have personalities as complex and different as people do." I propose that the same is true for learning and for the evaluation of it. For example, we know that learning occurs in various ways for different individuals and that no one method of instruction is best for all learning situations. There is widespread agreement that students have different learning styles and learn better from particular instructional modes and settings. Further, individualized instruction is more appropriate for teaching some subjects or skills to some learners, but group instruction can be more effective in other situations. "Different strokes for different folks" is a trite expression, I know. Nevertheless, it bears much importance in the evaluation of learning. Differences cannot be ignored.

I do not wish to imply, however, that we, as a profession, can be all things to all people. At times, we have to pass the buck to another office or department. We call it referral, and it is a vital function of many learning assistance programs. It is also an important by-product in the evaluation of learning. For instance, if we determine that our program and instruction are not the appropriate vehicles for meeting students' needs we try to send them to the place that can. This is good diagnosis and ultimately good practice in the evaluation of learning.

Keeping in mind that learning assistance programs are in the business of helping students become better learners and that we face very diverse populations, I submit that we must take an eclectic and individual approach to evaluating learning. I suggest that there is not one best method to evaluate learning as there is not one best method of instruction. There are, however, ideal combinations of methods, and these combinations vary according to individual learners. The evaluation approach I will present transcends individualized instruction and enables personalized evaluation of learning. It deals with the relationship of instruction to learning and allows for evaluating learners' needs and levels, which may result in decisions to provide large-, small-, or paired-group instruction.

In order to understand the rationale for choosing this approach, it is necessary to discuss some problems inherent in the evaluation of learning. Although there is a certain danger in beginning any discussion with problems, addressing them can lead to solutions. With this intent in mind, I shall proceed.

Problems in Evaluating Learning

Evaluation of learning in developmental or learning assistance programs is a relatively unexplored area. The professional literature on this subject does not abound with research studies. Most of the studies relate to the evaluation of learning assistance programs and not of learning. Much of what is reported has controversial findings that have been criticized extensively (Clymer, 1978; Dempsey, 1978; Santeusanio, 1974).

Defining and Communicating Terms. Defining evaluation terms has been a constant area of difficulty for evaluators (Popham, 1975). There is a tendency for evaluators to use terms interchangeably or not to define them at all. Thus, when a director announces to the staff that an outside evaluator is coming to assess the program's accountability, anxiety levels soar, sick days are taken, and colleagues stop talking to one another. Or when a student seeks assistance and is greeted with the announcement that his or her competencies will be measured, the student shudders, heads for the door, and never returns. Of course, these examples are exaggerated in that not everyone reacts in these ways, but evaluation and all of the terms that comprise it are threatening to many people.

Lack of understanding is part of the reason "evaluation" has a name that produces negative responses. Many times we are unsure of the purpose of the evaluation, and we are not certain of the improvements that will or have been made as a result of our participation. Braden and Walker (1978, p. 19) suggest: " 'evaluation' is a word we all use; therefore we think we know what it is. In reality, evaluation has so many different meanings . . . we cannot be sure that the other person is using *our* meaning . . . . It is the area of judgment that seems to produce the biggest hang-ups. No one wants to be the victim of judgment, final or temporary . . . . The tendency for the acts and issues of evaluation to become emotionally charged only complicates the problem of the diverse meanings given to the term."

This communication problem offers no solutions other than the hope that people involved with evaluation will read about evaluation theory and will learn and correctly use the most common definitions of the terms. Here are the major evaluation terms related to learning that will be used in this chapter and their commonly accepted definitions:

- *Evaluation:* "both a judgment on the worth or impact of a program, procedure, or individual and the process whereby that judgment is made" (Dressel, 1976, p. 1)
- *Measurement:* determining the degree to which an individual possesses a certain attribute with the assignment of some type of numerical index (Popham, 1975, p. 9)
- *Assessment:* "the process of gathering data and fashioning them into an interpretable form; judgments can then be made on the basis of this assessment" (Anderson and others, 1975, p. 27)
- *Testing:* "the act of gathering and processing evidence about human behavior under given conditions for purposes of understanding, predicting, and controlling future human behavior" (Bloom, 1970, p. 38).

Lack of Appropriate Instrumentation. A second problem that has plagued learning assistance practitioners, as well as educators in general, is the dearth of appropriate instruments with which to assess and measure learning. It is true that a smorgasbord of types of tests is available: achievement, aptitude, performance, criterion-referenced, inventories, and diagnostic. Further, of the tests at our disposal, the areas that they claim to measure are many: intelligence, self-concept, locus of control, study habits, learning styles, reading speed and comprehension, vocabulary knowledge, listening ability, writing ability . . . the list continues. There are teacher-made tests, competency tests, paper-pencil tests, oral tests, and demonstration tests. The proliferation of tests is great. That is not the problem. The problem for learning assistance programs is that they teach some skills for which there are few, if any, commercial tests available. Tests on listening comprehension, note taking, and reading-study textbooks come to mind. If there is no time to develop needed tests locally, then the practitioner often substitutes "the next best thing." For example, a standardized reading comprehension test is frequently the instrument used to assess students' abilities to read college material. When the Nelson-Denny Form C is used, the first selection requires the respondent to read a selection and answer questions about Greek mythology. The questions are written to test different levels of comprehension, but most of today's postsecondary developmental reading and study skills courses and learning centers go beyond the levels of reading comprehension (Maxwell, 1979). The Nelson-Denny Reading Test simply does not test a learner's ability to study and read textbooks, read and answer test questions, or take and study notes, yet these are often skills that are taught in developmental and learning assistance programs. The Nelson-Denny, and other norm-referenced tests are appropriate for screening those who might benefit from a developmental or learning assistance program, but they are inappropriate for determining the skill level that is necessary for achieving in postsecondary classrooms.

Misuse of Tests. The most pressing problem that we face is failure to utilize the tests for the purposes for which they were constructed. A survey of evaluation practices of 200 learning assistance programs in the United States (Clymer, 1978) revealed that 56.9 percent of the programs used standardized tests to evaluate the effectiveness of learning assistance programs. Of those same respondents, only 26.5 percent said that standardized tests gave them the most information regarding the effectiveness of the program. The most commonly used tests were the Nelson-Denny, McGraw-Hill Test of Basic Skills, Stanford Diagnostic Test, Iowa Silent Reading Test, and the California Achievement Test (Clymer, 1978, p. 70). Herein lies the essence of this crucial problem: These tests are all standardized, achievement, and norm-referenced tests. They have little capacity to evaluate a program's effectiveness because standardized tests are developed for comparisons of one individual to a group. Scores from such tests tell nothing more than how well one individual is achieving compared to others who have had the same number of years in school. Furthermore, the standardized test is constructed by giving the test to representative samples of students. If all respondents answer a question correctly, it is thrown out. Consequently, the test discriminates against the lower-level student. Hence, it is sometimes more of an intelligence test than an achievement test. Another symptom of this problem is that they are used to test achievement in specific, local curriculums, although they are designed to suit a general, national market. As a result, the tests are not suited to measure specific learning objectives. Certainly, a learning assistance program evaluator wants to assess these three components when evaluating program effectiveness, but the standardized test is not the appropriate measure (Maxwell, 1979; Popham, 1975; Smith, 1980). Most standardized tests are simply too general to evaluate the diversity that exists in learning assistance programs and in the population of learners they serve.

It is unfortunate that the majority of commercial tests available for purchase are inadequate for our needs in learning assistance. Moreover, in the context of evaluating learning, most tests, regardless of the type, "cannot tell what, how, or why students have learned nor the roles that antecedent learning and environmental factors have played in the learning process" (Wittrock, 1970, p. 9). Why then, the persistence in using standardized or other inappropriate tests to measure learning? Klein (1970, p.12) provides a logical reason: "Reliance upon and faith in the efficacy of testing have resulted mainly from the relative *efficiency* of tests as vehicles for providing *information for decisions* about students and the educational programs they receive . . . tests are almost always cheaper, quicker, fairer, and more valid and reliable information sources than are other assessment techniques such as interviews."

I belabor the inadequacy of the tests we have to measure learning. I observe many tests being misused in learning assistance programs. Research in the evaluation of learning has led to some promising alternatives to standardized tests. The remainder of this chapter will be devoted to describing these alternatives, as well as offering suggestions for the appropriate use of tests.

A Process for Evaluating Learning

Learning occurs every day, in many environments, and at many times. It has taken place since man first existed, or we would not be learning today. However, those who study learning have not been articulate on the topic of evaluation quite as long. *The Encyclopedia of Educational Evaluation* (Anderson and others, 1975, p. 143) credits Ralph W. Tyler "for the evaluation movement as we know it . . . ." His "major contribution was his insistence on defining the *goals and objectives* of programs in behavioral terms and making them the basis of instrument development and evaluation . . . ." His work "was particularly concerned with helping teachers formulate their objectives in order to improve their tests and adapt their instruction to the needs of individual pupils." While learning takes place in many instances that are not guided by needs, goals, and objectives (toddlers do not typically learn to talk as a result of mother's needs assessment and instructional plan), needs, goals, and objectives still have value in directing learning and effecting change in the behavior of learners.

Instruction and Learning: A Cause-and-Effect Relationship. A discussion of the evaluation of learning is not complete without comment on the relationship between instruction and learning. This is best described as a cause-and-effect relationship. Specifically, instruction is provided that will effect changes in a learner's behavior. According to Wittrock (1969), to evaluate instruction and the resultant learning that occurs, we can evaluate three aspects of learning and thereby evaluate instruction. The first aspect involves studying "the relationship between naturalistic learning environments and learners, on the one hand, and the criteria of learning on the other" (Wittrock, 1970, p. 17). The naturalistic learning environment, in Wittrock's (1969) view, includes such aspects as the time taken to accomplish the learning; the sequence of instruction; characteristics of the degree plan, the college classroom, the learning assistance center, and the library; and the training of instructors, tutors, peer counselors, or learning assistance facilitators. The second aspect of evaluating instruction via learning, is evaluating the "abilities, interests, and achievements [of learners] to determine student performance" (Wittrock, 1969, p. 3). The third aspect is to evaluate the changes in learning behavior as a result of instruction.

Hence, evaluation joins learning and instruction in that instruction is prescribed or planned on the basis of evaluating learners' entering abilities, interests, and achievements. Common terms that we use to evaluate learning prior to instruction are diagnosis, placement testing, or pretesting. Following instruction, changes in learners' abilities, interests, and achievements are evaluated. Labels we use for the evaluation of learning after instruction are competency testing, achievement testing, or posttesting. In learning assistance and developmental programs, far more evaluating on both ends of instruction occurs than in other areas of academe. Pretest, posttest and diagnosis, prescription, instruction, and evaluation are routines common to our profession.

Assessing Needs of Learners. In order to provide a learning environment that will be most effective, one must identify the needs of the learner and develop an appropriate instructional program. Identifying needs must be accomplished in an objective way. In other words, the evaluator must keep the learner's needs in mind at all times and try to make decisions based on those needs. Too frequently we establish programs that are based on our administrative and personal needs and preferences rather than on the learners' needs and preferences. One example of this is teaching everyone in a class the SQ4R method of study reading because we have found it effective or because it is easy to teach. Another example is not using any diagnostic tests because we do not like tests or cannot afford to purchase them. There are times when we have to use diagnostic tests. If there is no money for tests, it would be wise to learn to make tests locally and work with colleagues to develop them. Of course, budget constraints, political pressures, insufficient personnel, and lack of support from administration can cause us to compromise in providing an objective program, but sometimes our personal biases work against the best interests of the student. Implementation of informal and formal needs assessment techniques helps to maintain objectivity.

Areas of need in learning assistance programs fall into four basic categories: cognitive, affective, personal, and institutional. Examples and suggestions of informal and formal methods for determining needs are listed in Table 1. The table shows that needs assessment methodologies are similar in several areas and that program administrators could use the same techniques or instruments to identify a broad range of needs. For example, a learning assistance program that implements an initial interview or group survey can easily cover all four areas at the same time by asking the following:

- Circle the skill areas for which you need assistance.
- Do you like to read? Explain your answer.
- Describe your career goals.
- What is your academic status?

These questions would be asked on an interview form or information card for the student to answer the first time he or she used an individual program such as a learning center or a reading, writing, or math lab. Simi-

Table 1. Methods for Determining Learner Needs.

Area of Need	*Methodology*
Cognitive	
Learning skills	Administrater criterion-referenced and achievement tests; conduct surveys and interviews; make observations
Learning styles	Make cognitive maps; administer learning-style inventories
Learning habits	Administer habit inventories; conduct surveys, interviews
Intellectual ability	Make observations
Subject matter knowledge	Administer achievement tests, classroom tests, knowledge inventories; make observations
Affective	
Learning attitudes and values	Administer attitude, self-concept, personality inventories; make observations; conduct interviews
Personal	
Time	Make observations; conduct interviews
Career aspirations	Administer aptitude tests; conduct surveys, interviews
Finances	Review institutional records, conduct surveys
Family background	Review institutional records; conduct surveys, interviews
Extracurricular commitments	Conduct surveys, interviews
Institutional	
Entrance and good standing requirements	Review student records; conduct interviews
Degree and graduation requirements	Review student records; institutional catalogue; survey faculty
Department requirements	Review institutional catalogues, class syllabi; survey faculty

lar questions might appear on a survey form that is distributed the first day of a developmental reading, writing, or math class. Still other times an administrator will want to obtain a more global picture of the needs of students. A formal survey form or interview study might be instituted to assess needs in all categories and according to all levels: students, faculty, and administration.

Achievement, aptitude, and criterion-referenced tests; learning skills, attitude, and habit inventories; self-concept, personality, locus of control scales, and cognitive maps can help to further identify needs of students. Caution should be taken, however, in utilizing any of these instruments. Achievement and aptitude tests generally do not measure the specific cognitive needs of individual students; the instruments simply are not sensitive enough (Popham, 1975; Maxwell, 1979). Criterion-referenced tests are more sensitive to cognitive needs of individual learners because they assess ability according to specifically defined behavior domains. Unfortunately, questions concerning the validity and reliability of commercially produced criterion-referenced tests have been raised, and they are time-consuming to develop in-house (Popham, 1978). Inventories are quite valuable for identifying needs in the affective areas, but the respondent must give honest responses. In addition, few inventories have been tested for their validity (Popham, 1975). Regardless of the instrument, any test or inventory should be used to screen needs first and should be accompanied with some type of interview or counseling session so that the learner is provided with the opportunity to elaborate and explain responses and ask questions about the tests. Interviews will help the evaluator to identify needs more accurately.

Reviewing both student and institutional records within a program and outside of the program can help a learning assistance administrator gain information about needs in somewhat circuitous ways. Through an examination of records, the evaluator may observe that a student is on academic probation. Thus, a possible need can be identified. If the student does not want to remove probationary status, then there is little that anyone can do. However, if the student wants to achieve good academic standing, the need is identified. Examining records has greater value in the identification of patterns and trends of large groups of students. For example, the need to initiate a new program can be explored by analyzing which courses have high failure and attrition rates. The major difficulty with this type of needs assessment is time, of course. Where computers are available, the problem is more easily rectified.

Establishing the needs of individuals is a continual responsibility in the evaluation of learning. As some needs are met, new ones are identified. A learner improves in spelling and is ready to move into vocabulary building. Another learner begins to understand factoring and gets stuck with solving algebraic equations. Needs assessment is an ongoing process.

Diagnosis. One can hardly talk about needs in the evaluation of learning and not think of diagnosis. Diagnosis is refined observation or statement of the needs of the learner. The core of diagnosis is evaluating the learner's abilities, interests, and achievements, identifying strengths, weaknesses, and areas of recommended change. The result of this evaluation is most often an identification of instructional goals and behavioral or performance objectives.

Instructional goals are usually stated first in general or broad terms and are concerned with ultimate learning outcomes (Anderson and others, 1975, p. 179). Instructional objectives are more specific, short-range statements of intended learning behaviors. Finally, behavioral or performance objectives are stated in terms of measurable behaviors or performance. While some educators feel that behavioral objectives are too rigid (Anderson and others, 1975), they can help to focus instruction. This is especially important in basic skills programs where the needs of the learner are far below the level of achievement required for success in college.

The following are suggestions for diagnosis of student learning needs:

1. Diagnosis is not wrapped up and put back on the shelf after it is completed and instruction begins. It is an ongoing, cybernetic, integral part of instruction.

2. Interim goals and objectives sometimes need to be established for the learner in order to achieve the intended goals and objectives identified in the initial diagnosis. For example, the behavioral objective might be that the student will be able to spell 100 new words at the end of a semester. Possibly an interim objective would be established for the student to demonstrate knowledge of the most common rules in spelling before he or she could learn the 100 new words.

3. Diagnosis begins with some type of assessment, which varies according to the level of student and type of program. In many programs, it is a simple interview or discussion with the learner about his or her perceived needs. Students are frequently capable of diagnosing their own problems; they know them intimately, but do not put our educational labels on them. In other programs, diagnosis is an interview accompanied by certain diagnostic, criterion-referenced, or placement tests. Programs that are designed on the basis of large-group instruction often use standardized tests for initial diagnosis and screening, followed by specific diagnostic tests for those who do poorly on the standardized tests. Observation should be included with all types of diagnostic assessment to ensure that "no gap exists between obtaining information and using it" (Dempsey, 1978, p. 14).

4. In order to use observation effectively, good records must be kept on the student's progress, difficulties, successes, performance on activities, abilities, and feelings about activities. Essentially, observation helps the instructor to identify the learner's approach to a task, often revealing the affective influences in the learning.

5. Diagnosis of learning problems is not limited to assessing a learner's abilities, interests, achievements, strengths, and weaknesses. The academic environment must be considered as well, and the learning assistance staff must be familiar with the institutional politics that affect learning and the individual learner.

Prescription. Prescription is the result of evaluating the learning environment and deciding what activities, materials, length of time, and methods of instructional delivery the learner will need in order to accomplish the instructional goals and objectives. During prescription, the information gained through diagnosis must be incorporated into an instructional plan. For example, learners who have been mapped cognitively and demonstrate a high degree of audial learning preference should be given materials that require a large amount of listening ability. Further, the results of an informal reading inventory might show that several students are at the same level and can be grouped to learn basic word attack skills. A math placement test could indicate that most students need a review of percentages and fractions even though these areas are not included in the course objectives.

Prescription is largely trial-and-error, as I see it. One manipulates the learning environment until the desired changes in the learner's behavior occur. With some students, it takes several sessions or even semesters to pinpoint the cause of the learning difficulty and to arrange the learning environment appropriately so that the needed learning will occur. It is also common for unplanned learning to take place during the learning process, and the learning is usually welcomed by the instructor.

Some suggestions for prescribing the intended learning follow:

1. Prescribe materials and activities that will be interesting to the learner and that enhance his or her particular learning styles. In large-group instruction this is somewhat difficult; hence, one should try to vary methods of presentation or delivery of the material in order to meet the needs of a diverse group.

2. Record specific information about activities prescribed for each student in an individualized program. It is too difficult to remember what everyone is doing and when they should be doing it. Also, the records will serve as further diagnostic tools.

3. Ask students to informally evaluate the activities prescribed. Regularly assess the learning activities by obtaining the learner's perceptions of the interest and difficulty levels of the activities. This will enable the staff member to partially evaluate the instruction and thus immediately evaluate the learning environment.

4. Prescription is a continuous process like diagnosis. Diagnosis feeds into the prescription, which in turn directs the learning.

Methods of Evaluating Instruction and Learning

Because there is a cause-and-effect relationship between instruction and learning, it is necessary to discuss the evaluation of each process concurrently. Unfortunately, time does not permit a discussion of the topic of evaluation of instruction as it relates to teaching. Evaluation of instruction will be dealt with in the context of evaluation of learning, thus revealing the reciprocal nature of both processes.

Wittrock proposes (1969) that the evaluation of instruction occurs through the combined evaluation of learners, learning environments, and learning by relating the interactions of these learners, and the learning environmental characteristics to the learning. He contends that multivariate statistical procedures will enable us to measure the interactions involved in instruction and learning. While both multivariate statistics and a focus on instruction are beyond the scope of this paper, it is important to point out that the evaluation of learning is not an activity that can be accomplished in and of itself. When evaluating learning, one must consider many other factors that influence it. I do not suggest that all learning assistance evaluators can or should become familiar with multivariate statistics, but for those interested in this area of evaluation, these statistics are appropriate for studying learning. What I do offer, however, are some practical suggestions for evaluating the learner, the learning environments, the learning, and to some extent the interactions of those elements that go beyond the design of pre- and posttests.

Qualitative Methods of Evaluation. Michael Quinn Patton (1980) recently wrote that evaluation research is different things to different people and that if we answer all evaluation questions, we must understand the options available. Thus, eventually evaluation research will become a "paradigm of choices" (1980, p. 87). "A paradigm of choices" is the crux of qualitative, or what is sometimes called naturalistic evaluation, because the evaluator is not concerned with standardization. "Qualitative data consist of *detailed descriptions* of situations, events, people, interactions, and observed behaviors; *direct quotations* from people about their experiences, attitudes, beliefs, and thoughts; and excerpts or entire passages from documents, correspondence, records, and case histories . . . . Qualitative measures permit the evaluation researcher to record and understand people in their own terms. Qualitative data provide *depth* and *detail"* (p. 22).

Psychologists, sociologists, and anthropologists have been conducting qualitative research studies for years. Teachers, who are required to keep extensive records, are employing qualitative evaluation methods as well. Finally, learning assistance practitioners are aware of qualitative evaluation, as they have published many descriptions of programs in professional conference proceedings and yearbooks. Ironically, the authors of these articles have been criticized for these program descriptions (Bleismer, 1972; Emond, 1976). I do not question the criticism, because learning assistance professionals do not typically report the application of any statistics to the qualitative methodologies, but the great number of variables that influence learning in a college environment has forced evaluators of learning assistance to instinctively use qualitative methodologies. It is time to apply appropriate statistics to these methodologies.

Patton (1980) thoroughly discusses the subject of qualitative or naturalistic research in *Qualitative Evaluation Methods.* He provides information on using observation, interviews, and case studies; gathering data; and keeping records. He suggests that qualitative research be used in the following situations:

- Highly individualized, personalized, and humanistic programs
- Programs that serve diversified clientele
- Programs concerned with understanding and developing program processes, operations, and staff
- Programs concerned with improving the quality of the program and services it provides
- Administrators concerned with the inappropriateness of standardized measuring instruments and lack of valid measures due to many variables that influence the program
- Decision makers who are interested in evaluations that provide useful information (pp. 88-89).

In thinking about the professional literature that has been generated by the learning assistance and developmental education profession, in reflecting upon discussions I have had with colleagues at professional meetings, in remembering visitations to a variety of programs around the nation, and in knowing my own program, I believe that qualitative research has a home in learning assistance. We do not need to stop describing what our programs do and what our students are learning; we need to do a better job of it.

Combining Qualitative and Quantitative Research. Gains from pre- to posttest, increased GPA, and increased retention rates have been used to evaluate learning assistance programs since 1929 (Clymer, 1978). It can be assumed that although these measures were used to evaluate programs, an underlying purpose of the evaluations was to evaluate learning. The problems associated with these evaluations have been reported so extensively that it is redundant to repeat the difficulties here (Clymer, 1978; Emond, 1976; Maxwell, 1979). The reasons these measures are used are often out of the control of learning assistance administrators. Institutional administration, faculty, federal grant donors, lack of time and lack of appropriate instrumentation cause program personnel to continue to conduct studies based on these measures. When completing such studies for a variety of audiences, such as the administration, faculty, and federal agents, the limitations of these measures should be clearly identified. Maybe then they will not require them so earnestly. Lack of time is a relative problem that each administrator must contend with personally. Inappropriate instrumentation is a shortcoming of evaluation of learning in learning assistance that I would like to confront as I do believe there is a solution.

The solution comes from pitting the strengths of qualitative measurements against the weaknesses of quantitative measurements, and vice versa. The result is what I have called an eclectic approach to evaluating learning.

Putting this eclectic approach into practice begins with an assessment of the learner's achievements, abilities, interests, habits, and attitudes during his or her initial contact with the learning assistance program. This means interviewing or surveying the student first to see if the learning problem(s) can be diagnosed without subjecting the student to unnecessary tests. If needed, tests are administered and results are recorded, but observations of how the learner felt about the test and how it relates to the real learning situation should also be obtained and written down. These records will supply qualitative information that can support or refute the quantitative information from the test and help the evaluator to understand the affective variables that influence the test scores. Next, observing and keeping records of how the student interacts with the materials, activities, and learning environment provided permits continual evaluation of learning and instruction. Qualitative data from interviews and observations and the quantitative data from tests, GPAs, and attrition rates can be continually compared and analyzed informally or statistically to evaluate the cause-and-effect relationship of learning and instruction.

It is obvious that both qualitative and quantitative measures have limitations. The greatest limitation of qualitative measures is, of course, that they do not supply us with many numbers. Numbers are of great value to students. They like to see quantitative gains in scores on tests. These are motivating. Numbers also tell instructors how much time students are spending on the learning, and numbers enable administrators to know how many students are served and the cost of a program. This information certainly is applicable in evaluating the learning environment.

Quantitative measures are not sensitive to the day-to-day learning that occurs. It would be ridiculous to give students a test every day so that instruction could be constantly geared to their level; observation of how the student is applying the information is needed. If tests are constructed in-house to measure the instruction that has taken place or will take place in a particular learning assistance program, then they are probably adequate instruments for placing students. However, tests made by individuals outside the program generally have serious limitations for reasons stated previously.

Qualitative and quantitative measures must be used together to evaluate the complexities of the learner, the learning environment, the learning, and the instruction. Measures must be selected on the basis of the purpose of the evaluation, the characteristics of the learner, and the audience for whom the evaluation is intended. No single measure, qualitative or quantitative, is capable of evaluating the complexity of learning.

Selecting Appropriate Tests to Evaluate Learning. There are situations where it is absolutely necessary to evaluate learning via tests. It seems worthwhile to comment on specific criteria for selecting tests, to review their strengths and limitations, and to make recommendations for their use. Wayne Otto (1973) suggests that two basic questions must be posed when decisions about measurement instruments are being made: What do I want to know? and Does this instrument do the job? In response to the first question, if the practitioner merely wants to compare individuals in the program with larger groups of individuals or get a rough idea of the skill levels of students, then a standardized, norm-referenced achievement test is appropriate.

By contrast, if the evaluator wants to know the abilities of students at the times of entrance, exit, and throughout a program of instruction, a criterion-referenced test geared to the specific behavioral objectives should then be used. Although criterion-referenced tests are not abundant in the publishing market, several publications (Popham, 1975; Popham, 1978; Smith, 1980) specifically discuss the development and construction of such instruments.

In recent years, affective variables that contribute to learning have been researched. An outcome of this research is a variety of tests designed to measure the emotional and attitudinal influences on learning. This is a relatively new area of testing, and much progress has been made (Maxwell, 1979). Measures in this area are mostly of the inventory type but can supply a statement of an individual's perception of the relationship of attitudes, values, and interests to his or her learning. Difficulty with developing affective measures lies in the intangible nature of attitudes, values, and interests. Further, definitions of "appropriate" learning attitudes, values, and interests vary greatly among individuals; hence, they are not easy to observe or measure. Popham (1978) has suggested some promising methods for designing criterion-referenced instruments in the affective domain.

Because of the diversity of learning activities and the complexity of the mental processes that cause learning, researchers have been unable to devise instruments that measure all instructional objectives. Consequently, staff members have become involved with developing their own instruments to place students in a program and measure their achievement during and at the end of it. Such endeavors are extremely worthwhile if tests are geared directly to the instruction given and adhere to the basic guidelines of good test construction. (For a more detailed discussion of test design see Baker and Quellmalz, 1980.)

In answering the second question, "Does this instrument do the job?" the evaluator might use the following criteria to determine the adequacy of the measurement instrument:

Table 2. Tests and Appropriate Uses.

Type of Test	Strengths	Limitations	Suggestion for Use	References
Norm-referenced: tests that offer a comparison of an individual's performance with that of norm groups derived from large representative samples of individuals who have taken the same test under standardized conditions (Popham, 1978).	Can determine the ability of one student compared to a larger group locally or nationally. Useful for determining approximate skill levels of students. This helps with screening or selecting. Generally easy and quick to administer and score. Relatively economical. Wide variety available. Most have demonstrated reliability and validity.	Norming necessitates response variance. Response variance requires that some items responded to correctly by everyone must be discarded. It also causes ambiguous items to be included so that only the most capable examinees will respond correctly. Little diagnostic or predictive value since designed for groups rather than individuals, and there is little overlap with local objectives. Not sensitive to instruction: skills tested may rarely be used in local curriculums because of the general nature of test items. Cultural bias often present. Can yield inaccurate estimates of instructional levels because scores are based on the average of total scores, which is an arbitrary number. Time limits can be unrealistic. This penalizes slow-paced but "smart" students. Little value for low-ability student because tests often assume that students are beyond primary levels. Sometimes old test norms used if new editions aren't published. Interpretations can be difficult because of inadequate manuals.	Help students to understand the purpose of the test. To use for diagnosis, go beyond the numerical scores; follow up with an item analysis of mistakes and discuss errors verbally with examinee. Do not use to evaluate instruction—results will be invalid. Do not use only the test manual to interpret the results. Also use observations of student behavior outside of the testing situation. Note that the scores fall into a range because of the arbitrariness of the numerical equivalents. Stanine scores can be used here.	Bamman, 1970 Blanton, 1972 Grommon, 1976 Maxwell, 1979 Otto, 1973 Popham, 1975 Popham, 1978 Traxler, 1970
Criterion-referenced: tests that are used "to ascertain an individual's status with	No response variance is needed to make a test serve a general population. Can use to measure instruc-		Can be used to evaluate the effects of instruction and to make changes in the instruc-	Maxwell, 1979 Popham, 1975

Description	Advantages	Disadvantages	Recommendations	References
...domain" (Popham, 1975, p. 130).	...instructional planning. Specific learning skills can be directly measured. Test results provide descriptive information. Have potential to measure gains in the affective areas.	...Can't be used to evaluate the quality of instructional objectives. Retention and transfer of learning may be secondary.	...entative number of items (5 to 20) depending on the behavior domain (Popham, 1978). Use the test results to describe the status of an individual's learning and to prescribe further instruction. Can develop tests for affective behavior domains but the domain must be defined precisely; this can be difficult with attitudes, values, and interests.	1978 Smith, 1980 Traxler, 1970
Self-report inventories: instruments that are used to define a respondent's feelings, attitudes, interests, values, habits, or preferences regarding a specific subject.	Can use for assessment in affective areas. Relatively easy and economical to develop in a variety of areas. Inference and interpretations are often simple and obvious.	If answered untruthfully, results are useless. Reliability and validity are difficult to determine. Have limited value for evaluating the effects of instruction. Items can be ambiguous in an attempt to extract specific information.	Untruthful responses are less likely if the respondent doesn't know the purpose of the inventory. For easy interpretation, test results should be tabulated to present a diagram or map of examiner's perceived behavior. Good for counseling.	Maxwell, 1979 Popham, 1975 Robinson and Shaver 1975
In house measurements: informal tests, questionaires, checklists or inventories that are developed by program personnel for specific instructional purposes.	Can be directly geared to assess instructional objectives. Can be easily adapted to a specific population. Easy to administer.	Usually don't have reliability and validity. Objectivity can be difficult to develop. Can be time-consuming to develop.	Make a pilot test of the instrument before using it on a larger group. Include clear, concise directions. Determine and discard ambiguous or inappropriate items with continued use.	Otto, 1973

- The norms for a norm-referenced test should be derived from a a varied and representative population.
- A commercial test should be readily accessible, and easy to score and administer.
- The tests should be reliable and valid.
- The manual of a commercial test should be clearly written in terms of standardization, norming, and interpretation of information; directions for administering the test should be easy to understand and follow.
- The test should be economical.
- Alternate forms of commercial tests should be available for pre- and posttesting.
- The test should have an appropriate content for a local curriculum.
- The test should not be culturally biased.
- Before administering any test, the person who chose it should take the test to ensure that it is appropriate and adequate.

Unquestionably, tests can be of much value if they are used properly. Learning assistance practitioners would benefit from training and experience in test development and use, but they do not typically have the time to sift through the volumes of literature that exist on testing as it broadly applies to education. Table 2 categorizes and defines types of tests, identifies their advantages and disadvantages, offers suggestions for using them, and names some pertinent references in each category. One final note is that one test score is a relevant measure for only a specific moment in time. The test content, testing conditions, author of the test, and state of mind of the examinee all affect the final score, and there is very little finality about it; all of this could and probably would change tomorrow.

Conclusion

If we want to be a profession that truly assists students in learning, then we must take time to find out why they are not learning. Once we find that out, we can discover what they need to learn. Finally, we can discover what they in fact did learn as a result of participating in a learning assistance program.

To find answers to these questions, I have traced the relationship of learning evaluation to three interrelated components of the learning process: the learner, the learning environment, and instruction. I have presented and discussed an eclectic approach to evaluating the learning process that combines the collection of data from both qualitative and quantitative measures. Finally, I have identified shortcomings of tests used to evaluate learning and made suggestions for their appropriate utilization.

There is no one way to evaluate learning, and evaluation is not usually a quick and easy process. If we strive to find the best combinations of methods of evaluating learning for each student we serve, then we will be in a good position to help learners solve their learning problems. The buck may then stop at our open doors.

References

Anderson, S. B., Ball, S., Murphy, R. T. and Associates. *Encyclopedia of Educational Evaluation.* San Francisco: Jossey-Bass, 1975.

Baker, E., and Quellmalz, E. S. *Educational Testing and Evaluation.* Beverly Hills: Sage, 1980.

Bamman, H. A. "Assessing Progress in Reading. " In D. R. Farr (Ed.), *Measurement and Evaluation of Reading.* New York: Harcourt Brace Jovanovich, 1970.

Blanton, W., Farr, R., and Tuinman, J. J. (Eds.). *Reading Tests for the Secondary Grades.* Newark, Del.: International Reading Association, 1972.

Bleismer, E. P. "1971 Review of Research on College-Adult Reading." In F. P. Greene (Ed.), *Investigations Relating to Mature Reading: Twenty-First Yearbook of the National Reading Conference.* Vol. 1. Tampa, Fla.: National Reading Conference, 1972.

Bloom, B. "Toward a Theory of Testing Which Includes Measurement-Evaluation-Assessment." In D. C. Wittrock and D. E. Wiley (Eds.), *The Evaluation of Instruction: Issues and Problems.* New York: Holt, Rinehart and Winston, 1970.

Braden, R. A., and Walker, A. D. "Understanding Evaluation: Coping with a Communication Problem." *Audiovisual Instruction,* 1978, *23* (8), 19–20.

Christ, F. L. "Systems for Learning Assistance: Learners, Learning Facilitators, and Learning Centers." In F. L. Christ (Ed.)., *Interdisciplinary Aspects of Reading Instruction.* Proceedings of the Fourth Annual Conference of the Western College Reading Association, 1971.

Clymer, C. "An Analysis of Evaluation Practices of Learning Assistance Programs in Selected Institutions of the United States." Unpublished doctoral dissertation, Department of Curriculum and Instruction, New Mexico State University, 1978.

Dempsey, J. "Learning Assistance: Charting Our Course Within Reach." In G. Enright (Ed.), *Learning Assistance: Charting Our Course.* Proceedings of the Eleventh Annual Conference of the Western College Reading Association, 1978.

Dressel, P. L. *Handbook of Academic Evaluation: Assessing Institutional Effectiveness, Student Progress, and Professional Performance for Decision Making in Higher Education.* San Francisco: Jossey-Bass, 1976.

Emond, L. "The Status of Remediations in American Junior Colleges." A study prepared at Dean Junior College. *Resources in Education,* Sept. 1976.

Grommon, A. (Ed.). *Reviews of Selected Published Tests in English.* Urbana: National Council of Teachers of English, 1976.

Heard, P. "College Learning Specialists: A Profession Coming of Age." In R. Sugimoto (Ed.), *The Spirit of '76: Revolutionizing College Learning Skills.* Proceedings of the Ninth Annual Conference of the Western College Reading Association, 1976.

Klein, S. "Evaluating Tests in Terms of Information They Provide." *Evaluation Comment,* 1970, *2* (2), 1–6.

Maxwell, M. *Improving Student Learning Skills: A Comprehensive Guide to Successful Practices and Programs for Increasing the Performance of Underprepared Students.* San Francisco: Jossey-Bass, 1979.

Otto, W. "Evaluating Instruments for Assessing Needs and Growth in Reading." In W. H. MacGinite (Ed.), *Assessment Problems in Reading*, Newark, Del.: International Reading Association, 1973.

Patton, M. Q. *Qualitative Evaluation Methods*. Beverly Hills: Sage, 1980.

Popham, J. W. *Educational Evaluation*. Englewood Cliffs, N.J.: Prentice Hall, 1975.

Popham, J. W. *Criterion Referenced Measures*. Englewood Cliffs, N.J.: Prentice Hall, 1978.

Robinson, J. P., and Shaver, R. *Measures of Social and Psychological Attitudes*. Ann Arbor: Institute for Social Research, University of Michigan, 1975.

Santeusanio, R. P. "Do College Reading Programs Serve Their Purpose?" *Reading World*, 1974, *13*, 258–271.

Smith, K. G. "The Development and Analysis of a Criterion-Referenced Test of Textbook Reading and Vocabulary Discrimination for University Freshmen with Reference to Their ACT Scores." Unpublished doctoral dissertation, Department of Curriculum and Instruction, New Mexico State University, 1980.

Traxler, A. "Values and Limitations of Standardized Reading Tests." In D. R. Farr (Ed.), *Measurement and Evaluation of Reading*. New York: Harcourt Brace Jovanovich, 1970.

Wittrock, M. C. "The Evaluation of Instruction: Cause and Effect Relations in Naturalistic Data." *Evaluation Comment*, 1 (*4*), 1969, 1–7.

Wittrock, M. C. "The Evaluation of Instruction: Cause and Effect Relations in Naturalistic Data." In M. C. Wittrock and D. E. Wiley (Eds.), *The Evaluation of Instruction:Issues and Problems*. New York: Holt, Rinehart and Winston, 1970.

Carol Clymer Walvekar is the assistant director of study skills and tutorial services at the University of Texas at El Paso.

Performance evaluation serves as an invaluable tool
for maximizing the potential of staff by providing
them with feedback on previous performance and
guidance for professional development.

Staff Performance Evaluation in Learning Assistance Centers: A Key to an Efficient and Effective Program

Karen G. Smith
Susan C. Brown

As educators and learning assistance practitioners, we proclaim the value—indeed, the necessity—of evaluating our students' learning skills development and the efficacy of our programs and services. We evaluate our cost-effectiveness and our relationships with other academic departments. We evaluate our image and our effectiveness in public relations. We evaluate our instructional materials and our teaching methods. And we evaluate ourselves and the job performance of our staff.

The need for change, adaptation, development, and innovation is demonstrated and determined by and through evaluation, both formal and informal. Historically, learning assistance programs were initiated as the need for such academic support programs in colleges and universities was demonstrated through campus-wide assessment. These programs have grown, taken on new dimensions, and adapted or expanded the original

C. C. Walvekar (Ed.), *New Directions for College Learning Assistance: Assessment of Learning Assistance Services*, no. 5. San Francisco: Jossey-Bass, 1981.

services as appraisal demonstrated the practicality and profitability of such change for the learners and for the institution.

Just as learning assistance program development has grown and matured, so have our skills in program assessment and learner evaluation. Our knowledge and skills in conducting staff evaluation and development, however, have generally not developed and matured commensurate with our other abilities in evaluation. A well-developed performance evaluation system is at the heart of an effective human-resource management system (Newman and Hinrichs, 1980); therefore, performance evaluation is one key to an effective and efficient learning assistance program.

Drucker (1964) has referred to professional workers as "knowledge workers." They are usually crucial to innovation and productivity in the organization, and they are the "gatekeepers of important information, the designers of new products and systems, the drivers of productivity" (Newman and Hinrichs, 1980, p. 4). The professional positions in learning assistance programs represent high institutional investments and high payoff potential in the delivery of learner services. Since the program director's job is to get things done through others—to achieve the program's goals through the job performances of the staff—it is clear that performance evaluation through appraisal and development is a central part of the director's overall task of performance management.

An effective performance evaluation process is designed to provide support for effective performance, which is a critical component for sustaining motivation, attracting top skill, and preventing turnover. Performance evaluation, in essence, serves two basic purposes: (1) the appraisal of staff performance and progress toward individual and organizational goals and (2) the development of employee potential, performance, and commitment. Cummings and Schwab (1973) define the two purposes as the maintenance of organizational control and the efficiency with which the organization's human resources are being utilized and developed. Stated yet another way, performance evaluation rewards those who perform outstandingly and assists those who do not perform well (Ripple, 1981).

Goals and Objectives

Program evaluation is easiest and most useful when it is tied to goals and objectives that are clearly stated, in measurable form, and prioritized. Performance goals and objectives for the employee are most beneficial when they relate directly to the organizational mission, goals, and objectives.

Organizational Mission, Goals, and Objectives. A mission statement is an expression of "general intent, usually in the form of a policy; it applies to the system as a whole over a long period of time" (American Association of School Administrators, 1973, p. 36). A goal is a statement that describes a terminal point to be reached in order to fulfill the mission and that provides general direction to pursue the mission. Etzioni (1964), an early proponent of the use of organizational objectives, describes an organizational goal as a desired state of affairs that the organization attempts to bring about as a collectivity. Drucker (1964) identifies three kinds of organizational goals: (1) additive goals, which more fully exploit already existing resources; (2) complementary goals, which change the structure of the organization by combining a new dimension with an old; and (3) breakthrough goals, which change the fundamental characteristics and capacity of the organization.

Objectives are outcome statements that are consistent with a related goal statement. Objectives are more specific expressions of a behavior, process, or product to be achieved over a shorter time period (American Association of School Administrators, 1973). An objective is a description of an end result to be achieved. The organizational objectives outline the steps required to reach the goals. Essential points to remember in writing the organizational goals and objectives are that they must be challenging, attainable, measurable, and supportive of the organizational mission.

When the organizational management system is based on stated goals and objectives, when the priorities are established, when time lines are set, and when all can and will be measured, then management by objectives (MBO) is the organizational management system utilized. McConkey (1975) outlines four steps in MBO for nonprofit organizations. First, the program manager, with input from staff, determines the mission, goals, and objectives for the organization. Next, each employee states areas of responsibility, long-term goals, specific objectives, and measures of acceptable results for his or her position. Then the objectives of personnel and of the organization are blended and balanced to achieve the optimum in results. Finally, a control mechanism is initiated to monitor progress toward both the organizational and individual objectives, and each person's results are measured.

Performance Objectives. The establishment of individual performance objectives is based on two related concepts (Cummings and Schwab, 1973). First, when the objectives to be reached are determined by the employees, they know what they are trying to accomplish, and their chances of accomplishing the objectives are good. Second, progress can only be measured in terms of what one is trying to make progress toward.

Employee goals and objectives are important determinants of individual performance. Migliore (1977) states that after employees have participated in setting goals and objectives, they feel committed. However, employees will not commit themselves to an organization unless they know what the organization wants from them and what kinds of rewards they will receive (Grant, 1981).

Performance objectives should include some of each of three kinds: routine, problem-solving, and innovative. Routine, or regular, objectives are ongoing and can be expected to continue to be an integral part of the job. The routine objectives serve to provide the employee with a sense of security, predictability, and stability in reference to the job. Problem-solving objectives are set in order to provide or develop solutions to problems, to restore normalcy, and to correct or solve job or organizational problems. Problem-solving objectives require employees to use their skills and knowledge, to take initiative, and to employ creative thinking strategies. Innovative objectives allow employees the opportunity to be creative, to follow their special interests as they relate to the job.

Odiorne (1971) states that setting creative or innovative objectives is imperative in order to eliminate the status quo and boredom with the job. Odiorne identified two categories of innovative objectives: (1) extrinsic creativity, which is the application, adaptation, and implementation of new technology, instruction, techniques, or methods that were developed elsewhere, and (2) intrinsic innovation, which allows employees to design, invent, and initiate a product, process, or system created by their own knowledge, skills, and interests.

Performance objectives are part of the management system; they aren't the system itself. Without an effective management system that facilitates writing the objectives and translates them into practice, performance objectives are worthless.

The management system should include the following steps (McConkey, 1975):

1. Determining organizational mission, goals, objectives, priorities, and ground rules

2. Defining job purpose and responsibility

3. Determining areas of key results

4. Initiating job analysis

5. Writing performance objectives

6. Coordinating individual performance objectives with others and with the organizational mission, goals, objectives and priorities

7. Tailoring feedback to performance objectives

8. Developing a plan for individual behavior change or behavior modification, and for growth; and

9. Repeating the process each year.

Writing performance objectives need not be viewed as a formidable task. An excellent list of criteria to be used as a guide when writing performance objectives is provided by McConkey (1975). A summary of the criteria is provided here.

Priorities. Performance objectives should direct effort and energy toward priority outcomes established by the individual as those outcomes relate to the organizational priorities. Employee motivation and personal commitment can be wasted and lost if the individual's work efforts are inappropriately directed toward objectives that are of minor or no importance to the organizational mission. Clear communication and feedback must be included in the objective-writing process so that organizational and individual priorities are fused into the performance objectives.

Specificity. The objectives must be as specific and measurable as possible. They should tell what (the end result) and when (a target date or a target period). Vague and ambiguous terms that should be avoided include: reasonable, justifiable, maximum, allowable, highest, lowest, best, desirable. The objectives should be defined in terms of observable behavioral outcomes, with the critieria specified by which the attainment of the objective is to be judged.

Attainability. It is self-defeating for the manager and the employee to set unrealistic objectives or to refuse to revise them if subsequent events demonstrate that the objectives were based on false assumptions or if unsurmountable problems are encountered. Performance objectives should be viewed and used as a living, viable means of managing. As such, performance objectives, and the plans for achieving them, should not be viewed as unchangeable or totally inflexible.

"Stretch." If continual improvement of the program and of the individual employee's performance is a given in the learning assistance program, then performance objectives should be set at a level of difficulty and achievement that will require the staff member to exert more than minimum effort. Essentially, the determination of stretch will be based on the manager's and employee's evaluation of the employee's capabilities, drive, motivation, and past record and of the performance levels of others in parallel positions.

Match with Experience and Capability. One of the major virtues of performance evaluation is that it can serve as a means of personal and, also, of organizational development. However, in order for this benefit to be realized, the complexity and difficulty of the objectives should be matched to the experience and capability of the employee. If the objectives are set too high, they can lead to frustration, anger, and lack of personal development. If set too low, they can demotivate, initiate boredom, and lead to loss of job commitment.

Responsibility and Authority. All objectives should cover activities and results for which the individual has the responsibility and the necessary authority to carry them to fruition. Careless wording of the objectives can easily result in assuming authority and responsibility that actually do not exist for the employee.

Updating. Typically, the target period in college and university programs is the semester or quarter unit, the academic year, or the fiscal year. Normally, problem-solving and innovative objectives should change from period to period, while routine objectives may remain constant from one target period to the next. The rewriting and changing of objectives from one target period to the next helps to prevent the perpetuation of obsolete programs and activities. It also helps to ensure that employees continue to address their efforts to constantly changing their priorities and needs as determined by the institutional and organizational climate and learner needs.

Number of Objectives. There is no set recommended number of objectives for all employees. Ordinarily, the program manager and program supervisors, who are responsible for not only their own work but for the work results of others, would set more objectives than the employee who has a narrow set of responsibilities. Probably a maximum of five to seven major problem-solving and innovative objectives, plus the routine objectives that relate to regular job responsibilities, would be a good rule of thumb (McConkey, 1975).

Vertical and Horizontal Compatibility. Since performance objectives are not an end in themselves nor are they written in the exclusivity of an autonomous position, they must be compatible with and help carry out the objectives of the organizational unit (vertical compatibility). They must also be supportive of and mesh with the objectives of parallel staff members (horizontal compatibility).

Wording of Objectives. Contrary to the advice of some educational and management writers, the actual wording or format that will cover the multiplicity of performance objectives evolving from the many units and levels of an organization is not a crucial issue. Even though vague terms should be avoided, primary emphasis should be devoted to the inclusion of the criteria previously discussed.

Performance Appraisal

A first step toward implementing performance evaluation is the job analysis, which is usually conducted by the manager or by the manager and employee together (Davies, 1981). Questions to be answered in the job analysis are: What has to be done? How can (should) it be accomplished? When should it be initiated and completed? Where does this occur? What level of skill, or standard, is required? What level is expected? Answers to these questions form the basis for the job description. They also provide the basis for the routine, the problem-solving, and the innovative performance objectives, and thus, the performance appraisal. The job analysis will systematically reduce the probability of human error occurring because of unclear or nonexistent guidelines.

Performance evaluation based on organizational and individual objectives supports the process of knitting together the employee and the organization through communication and mutual adjustment. Performance evaluation is not, according to Moravec (1981), merely telling an employee about his or her past performance. It is, he advises us, continuous performance planning, communication, evaluation, and development.

Performance criteria may be classified into three general categories: (1) the actual job behaviors of the employee, (2) the results and outcomes of those job behaviors, and (3) the impact of those outcomes and behaviors on organizational effectiveness.

Performance appraisal, in order to be effective and meet legal requirements, is most easily conducted when it is based on performance objectives that were written in terms of observable behavioral outcomes. In other words, the objectives should state the criteria by which the attainment of the objective is to be measured. Changes in attitude, perspective, or understanding are meaningless unless they result in improved job behavior.

Focusing on behavior achieves several things (Smith and Brouwer, 1977). First, eliminating personality judgments during the appraisal discussion and focusing on observations of behavior provide a more readily acceptable appraisal situation to the employee. Second, dealing with data that both the manager and employee can observe eliminates employee defensiveness. Third, identifying specific actions that can be changed establishes a base for the employee's developmental plan for the future. Finally, emphasizing observable behavior outcomes in the appraisal process allows the manager to be as objective as is humanly possible.

The definition of objectives in terms of observable behavioral outcomes applies to the process used, as well as to the end results. Most managers recognize that the way the results are achieved has important consequences for the organization. This is of particular concern in organizations that deal with the welfare, development, or health of people. Learning assistance program managers are especially concerned with the humanistic qualities of personnel—how they relate, how they teach, how they counsel. The process by which things get done affects the vitality of our programs fully as much as the ability to accomplish our goals and objectives. Trust, communication, and innovative thinking are critical to our programs and should be fostered through employee performance appraisal and development. They can be observed through observable behavior outcomes and through process, as well.

A number of procedures can be incorporated in the appraisal process. The most common of these is the supervisory appraisal of the employee. A second procedure is a peer appraisal process, which may be seen as less threatening to the employee being appraised because of a higher level of trust. A third type is a self-appraisal, which is especially important for the development of the individual. A self-appraisal, completed independently and prior to the supervisor's appraisal, provides an excellent vehicle for communication. It is particularly important to note differences in rating that may indicate where the goals of the organization and the goals of the individual vary. In general, a self-evaluation allows for personal growth and enables the employee to have input in the appraisal process. A fourth type of appraisal is completed by subordinates. Generally, this type is completed anonymously to allow for a more honest rating. It is important to remember, however, that subordinates who have not been trained in evaluation may not have a sophisticated understanding of the goals of an organization and may tend to evaluate personalities rather than performances. Each of these types of appraisals provides a different perspective, and together they help to paint a total picture (Cummings and Schwab, 1973).

Communication. Performance appraisal is based on continuous communication and feedback. Regular meetings should occur between manager and each employee to go over progress toward objectives and goals. As critical incidents occur, the manager provides immediate feedback. Although the manager is aware that people may make mistakes, he or she must also be aware that they will not necessarily learn from these mistakes. Therefore, employees need continuous communication regarding their performance. The annual performance appraisal session should contain no surprises; rather, it should be a total summary and integration of the preceding year.

Managers must give feedback to employees, but to make the communication process complete, employees must reciprocate. Employees tend to hesitate in sharing information on manager performance, especially if it is negative. An effective manager, therefore, tries to obtain all relevant information. He or she is receptive to both positive and negative criticism, listens carefully, and responds in an accepting way, without defensiveness. The manager must be aware that others have equally valid ideas and that there may be more than one way of accomplishing a goal. However, after the manager has received feedback and completed the communication process, he or she must ultimately be responsible and accountable for carrying out the organizational objectives.

Appraisal Interview. During the appraisal, the manager must allot enough time without interruptions. It is important to listen to what the employee is saying and to respond. As the performance is reviewed, the manager should give the employee examples of behavior based on specific incidents, not on hearsay. The manager should explain what is wrong with the work, not with the person. Honest feedback is essential, for it allows the person being evaluated to change behavior and improve. Overlooking unacceptable behavior is doing an injustice to an employee. Generally, people can accept constructive criticism that is out in the open.

In evaluating an employee, Smith and Brouwer (1977) point out the importance of keeping in mind the value system of the organization and the quality of performance. Assume, as an example, that teamwork is a value of the organization. If, on one hand, a top producer exhibits no teamwork, but alienates co-workers, then the manager must be careful to point out the employee's lack of teamwork. Otherwise, the employee will continue to produce at the expense of the team. On the other hand, an employee who may not be a top producer but who has the capability of developing cohesiveness among his or her co-workers should be rewarded for the ability to work productively on the team.

Employee Development

Frequently, performance evaluation ends with the performance appraisal interview. In order for it to be truly beneficial to both the organization and the employee, the performance evaluation should be used as a springboard for employee development. Although commenting on past performances is important, the real value of the system is to plan for future employee development. The appraisal interview provides information on which to base salary and promotion, provides for organizational planning, and provides feedback to the employee from which developmental objectives can be formulated. The developmental meeting uses that information to expand and maximize individual employee potential.

The appraisal interview and the developmental meeting for setting new performance objectives are most productive if they are held at two separate times, with the developmental meeting following soon after the appraisal meeting. Managers have difficulty in being both judge and counselor at the same time, and, while the appraisal interview is essentially a judgmental interview, the developmental interview is a counseling interview. The role of judge is generally not a comfortable one, and managers tend to have difficulty giving negative feedback to employees. For example, including discussion of the developmental objectives during the appraisal interview may lead the manager to gloss over the appraisal of performance since both manager and employee may find it more comfortable to focus on planning for the future. The employee deserves the opportunity to fully understand the appraisal of performance and all of its implications before making new plans. When the manager criticizes employee behavior, the employee may feel upset or need time to think about and respond to the evaluation. Emotional reactions may make it difficult to focus on developmental plans. A constructive appraisal interview allows plenty of time for discussion, feedback, and negotiation for both the manager and the employee (Smith and Brouwer, 1977).

The meeting for setting the developmental objectives ideally occurs soon after the appraisal meeting in order to ensure that areas of concern are fresh to both manager and employee. In preparation for this meeting, the employee may be asked to consider the evaluation and formulate several personal job performance objectives for the coming year. Using the performance appraisal, the employee's objectives, and the manager's constructive ideas for the employee, the manager and employee together formulate a developmental plan that considers both organizational and individual needs and includes the three types of objectives: routine, problem-solving, and innovative. The objectives are geared toward production as well as maximizing employee potential and strengthening areas that were pinpointed in the appraisal interview as weak. Objectives should also relate to the employee's career goals. Employee input in all of the objectives, especially in the area of personal growth and development, ensures a deeper commitment. Through negotiation and discussion, the objectives are established and written in detailed language that communicates the specific expected results. With the objectives is a time frame that indicates when the achievement of each goal is expected.

Employee development is a continuous process, occurring all year long. The effective manager is interested in the full staff potential, both personally and professionally. The developmental meeting provides an important opportunity for motivating the employee and establishing a fresh start. If performance evaluation is conducted with these factors in mind, it becomes a positive and exciting experience for both manager and employee.

Behavior Change

Effective development demands change through new action, expanded action, or adapted action. The role of the manager is to facilitate change in behavior. To do this, the responsive manager must be aware of psychological factors affecting behavior change. All behavior can be seen as directed toward meeting needs. Although the needs may be perfectly legitimate, employees may be using unacceptable or unproductive ways of meeting them. A manager can assist the employee in learning more acceptable or more productive ways of meeting those needs.

Self-Concept. It is necessary to be aware that how employees view themselves determines the methods used to meet their needs. A manager, by being sensitive to an employee's self-concept, can facilitate a change in perception, which in time will change the behavior (Smith and Brouwer, 1977). It is often necessary to look beyond the outward unacceptable behavior to the inner need toward which it is directed. As an example, a defensive employee may have a need to be perfect. The manager can assist this employee by helping him or her to see and accept the fact that no one is perfect. The employee needs to be reinforced for listening to others and for being flexible. Through positive reinforcement of the underlying need, change can take place.

Intrinsic/Extrinsic Rewards. Change in behavior can also be facilitated through rewards. There are two types of rewards: intrinsic and extrinsic. Intrinsic rewards are self-rewards, such as the personal satisfaction of having completed a job to the best of one's abilities. Extrinsic rewards, such as pay raises, promotions, and so forth, are given by others. Although pay raises and promotions are not always available to managers in educational institutions, other types of extrinsic rewards may be of equal value. Opportunities for professional growth, such as conference attendance, workshop attendance, development of materials, expansion of professional areas of expertise, presentation of papers, and special-interest projects, can all be extrinsic rewards. While offering extrinsic rewards to achievers, the effective manager facilitates the development of intrinsic rewards by providing opportunities for the employee to experience success. Once the employee has experienced the positive effects of success, he or she will attempt to do well in similar situations. The confidence gained will also enable the employee to "stretch" for new experiences.

Although extrinsic rewards are necessary, it is extremely important that employees not be dependent on these rewards. The typical postsecondary system does not allow for pay raises or promotions. In addition, receiving extrinsic rewards may leave the employee feeling unmotivated or empty inside, which may result in a loss of production. The reason for this is that upon achieving the goal that the employee has worked toward, he or she may experience a void or a feeling of loss, since there is nothing left to work toward.

Intrinsic rewards, however, are self-produced and, as such, are unending. Receiving them does not cause a void but motivates the employee to want greater achievement. The greater the amount of intrinsic rewards a person receives, the more satisfied he or she will be with the job. In order for a reward system to be successful, the rewards offered must be of value to the employee. It is also important that rewards be offered to those who achieve the highest, because if high achievers are not rewarded, others will lose incentive.

Role Modeling. Another method for encouraging behavior change is through role modeling. This is a continuous process frequently overlooked by the manager. Managers must look at the role model they are projecting to their staff. As an example, if the manager feels that punctuality is important, then the manager should be on time. If creativity is important then the manager should demonstrate personal innovation and acceptance of creativity. The manager, through his or her example, is a key factor in facilitating behavior change by allowing participation in determining goals, by providing appropriate rewards, and by being aware of employees' needs. Too frequently, these elements are overlooked in dealing with employees.

Methodology

Elements. The following five elements should be included in the performance evaluation (Salloway and Dayton, 1981). These elements may be subdivided in any manner in order to effectively appraise the performance of the employee, as measured against the employee's performance objectives.

1. *Capacity:* The ability to use personal education and knowledge in application toward job responsibilities and toward the realization of performance objectives is an indication of employee capacity.

2. *Activities:* The identification of specific accomplishments in independent work and in activities with others gives a measure of individual performance. The effectiveness of work relationships with peers, subordinates, and supervisors is also indicated in this element of performance.

3. *Impact:* The individual's influence (positive or negative) on the total success of the organization and on the organizational goals is an element sometimes overlooked by the evaluator.

4. *Ability to manage:* The employee's demonstration of skills in planning, making reports, completing required tasks, and realizing completion of his or her objectives is an important element in performance evaluation.

5. *Personal attainments:* The realization of personal and professional goal accomplishments measures employee drive and motivation and also affects the visibility and viability of programs in higher education.

Criteria/Standards. In choosing the appropriate criteria of performance, the manager must first determine which aspects of performance should be evaluated. Newman and Hinrichs (1980) suggest that performance criteria must be valid, reliable, practical, and multidimensional. First, validity: the performance criterion must be relevant to the individual and to the organization. Neither the criterion nor the measure of it should be trivial. In other words, relevancy demands that the goal to be judged and also the measure of the goal achievement have validity. Second, the performance criterion needs to demonstrate reliability; that is, to be stable and measurable. Specifically, evaluation of a given performance criterion should be in agreement over time and with different evaluators. Important determinants of reliability are observability and objectivity in the appraisal process. Third, the measurement of performance must be practical, usable, and acceptable to those who administer it and to those whose decisions will be based on it. Finally, the responsibilities and expectations of professional staff in learning assistance are generally broad and multidimensional. A single measure of success or failure is extremely unlikely. Effective job performance likely involves behaving competently in a number of different dimensions. To achieve both purposes of performance evaluation—appraisal and development—it is important to assess each and every critical dimension of performance.

Methods of Appraisal. Over the years, several appraisal methods have emerged in the management field. These methods cluster as variations of four general types: comparative procedures, absolute standards, direct indexes, and management by objectives (Cummings and Schwab, 1973).

Comparative Procedures. These methods are characterized by two features: evaluation is made by comparing one employee against other employees on the element of interest, and the comparison is usually made on one global dimension of the employee's overall effectiveness to the organization. Comparative procedures include three procedures that rank all employees and a fourth that is a forced distribution procedure.

Straight ranking identifies among all the employees the best performer, the next best, and so on. In alternative ranking, the manager identifies the best performer from an alphabetical list of all employees, then the poorest, then the next best, the next poorest—alternating between thinking of the best and poorest employee. In the paired comparison technique, each employee is compared to every other employee, one at a time. The employee's final ranking is determined by how many times he is chosen over other employees. When the fourth comparative appraisal technique, forced distribution, is used, a certain percentage of the total employees must be assigned to each of several factors; that is, 10 percent of the employees highest on a factor, 20 percent above average, and so forth.

Obvious limitations are evident in comparative evaluation procedures. Usually employees are compared, regardless of which of the four techniques is used, on only one dimension, usually some global-effectiveness measure. It seems highly unlikely that one general characteristic can be identified as indicative of job success. Another difficulty lies in problems with comparing two or more groups of rankings. For instance, two supervisors who must evaluate job performance on individuals with split assignments may have great difficulty in merging their individual appraisals of the employees into one. The most serious limitation of comparative evaluation procedures pertains to the difficulty of using ranking procedures for developmental and feedback purposes. The rankings provide only a very generalized appraisal with little concrete evidence for improving performance. Also, the act of appraisal based on comparison generates a tone of being "better" or "worse" than other employees and leads to the tendency to discuss personalities rather than job behaviors in the appraisal interview.

Absolute Standards. Appraisal systems that use absolute standards are differentiated from comparative systems in two ways. First, each individual is evaluated against several written standards rather than against other employees. Second, several elements of performance are usually measured rather than one global dimension. In absolute standards methods, the employee is described as either having or not having the performance characteristic or he is described as having each characteristic to a particular degree. The critical incidents method of absolute standards requires that each employee be evaluated on specified requirements that are critical to the successful performance of the job. This procedure also demands that the manager identity positive or negative incidents that occur pertaining to the general categories. Another absolute standards procedure is the weighted checklist, which assigns values of weight to descriptive statements about employee performance on the job to be rated. The manager then appraises each employee's performance by indicating whether he or she does or does not engage in the behavior specified in each item. The total sum of the scores of the items checked for the employee determines the overall appraisal score (Cummings and Schwab, 1973). Rating scales appear in many forms but generally present several statements about job behavior and a continuous or discrete scale upon which each employee is appraised.

Direct Indexes. This method provides information about performance without the necessity of the performance behavior being appraised by an evaluator. Direct measures are generally most appropriate on jobs with easily definable outcomes. Two such indexes are measures of productivity and job withdrawal. Measures of productivity attempt to measure individual performance through the collection of quality data (hours of output, monthly gross sales, number of students with increased GPA, number of student "repeats"). Measures of withdrawal are demonstrated by actual job attendance, another form of productivity. Direct indexes as appraisal processes have more relevant application in industry than in education systems.

Management by Objectives. MBO is an alternative to employee comparison and conventional rating systems (McGregor, 1960). Because of its positive elements as not only a performance appraisal tool but also as a management technique for employee development, this method has been presented by the authors as the most relevant and positive performance evaluation method to be used in learning assistance programs. In review, first the employee objectives, specific and measurable, are identified. Next, the objective is carried out by the employee. Third, the employee's performance against the objectives initially established is appraised. And, finally, new objectives and a plan for employee development within the subsequent time period are established.

Conclusion

Performance evaluation is a managerial tool that provides the employee with direction, feedback, appraisal, and developmental assistance. It nurtures competency, growth, motivation, reward, teamwork, promotion, training, and accountability. Odiorne (1971) points out that the use of employee performance objectives (1) eliminates the possibility of activity overcoming the goal, (2) defines success in specific output terms, (3) improves overall organization and performance, and (4) achieves individual improvement and growth.

The effective manager is a crucial element to the successful implementation of performance evaluation for appraisal and development. He or she must know and understand the employees and be aware of their needs. The manager must have a good understanding of the psychology of behavior and how to effect behavior change. With these skills, the effective manager can facilitate the development of maximum potential of each employee through performance evaluation.

References

American Association of School Administrators. *Management by Objectives and Results.* Arlington, Va.: American Association of School Administrators, 1973.

Cummings, L. L., and Schwab, D. P. *Performance in Organizations: Determinants and Appraisal.* Glenview, Ill.: Scott, Foresman, 1973.

Davies, I. "Task Analysis for Reliable Human Performance." *Performance and Instruction,* 1981, *20* (2), 8–10.

Drucker, P. F. *Managing for Results.* New York: Harper & Row, 1964.

Etzioni, A. *Modern Organizations.* Englewood Cliffs, N.J.: Prentice-Hall, 1964.

Grant, P. C. "How to Manage Employee Job Performance." *Personnel Administrator,* August 1981, pp. 59–65.

McConkey, D. D. *MBO for Nonprofit Organizations.* New York: American Management Associations, 1975.

McGregor, D. *The Human Side of Enterprise.* New York: McGraw-Hill, 1960.

Migliore, R. H. *MBO: Blue Collar to Top Executive.* Washington, D.C.: Bureau of National Affairs, 1977.

Moravec, M. "How Performance Appraisal Can Tie Communication to Productivity." *Personnel Administrator,* January 1981, pp. 51–54.

Newman, J. E., and Hinrichs, J. R. *Performance Evaluation for Professional Personnel.* Scarsdale, N.Y.: Work in America Institute, 1980.

Odiorne, G. S., "Management by Objectives." *College and University Journal,* 1971, *10,* 13–15.

Ripple, G. G. "Appraising Performance." *The College Board Review,* Spring 1981, p. 119.

Salloway, R. J., and Dayton, A. S. "Personal Scorecards for the Overloaded Financial Officer." *Management Focus,* July-August, 1981, pp. 28–32.

Smith, H. P., and Brouwer, P. J. *Performance Appraisal and Human Development.* Reading, Mass.: Addison-Wesley, 1977.

Karen G. Smith is the designer, developer, and director of the Center for Learning Assistance at New Mexico State University, where she received her M.A.T. and Ed.D. degrees. She is an instructor in reading education courses and has served as a consultant in learning skills, learning assistance, and management skills to New Mexico public school districts and six New Mexico institutions of higher education.

Susan C. Brown is coordinator of Outreach Services at the Center for Learning Assistance, New Mexico State University. She has designed and coordinated staff training programs, innovative degree courses, and special nontraditional student programs for university learning assistance centers and support services. She has a doctorate in curriculum and instruction with emphasis in college reading.

Evaluation is a tool for solving problems that result from an ever-changing educational environment.

Concluding Comments

Carol Clymer Walvekar

Evaluation is a common element in learning assistance programs. The role and application of evaluation vary as much as programs do, but it is likely that evaluation exists in almost every program at some level and to some degree. It is not apparent why one program comprehensively evaluates most aspects of its program, from staff to the learning environment, and another evaluates instruction only, or why one administrator has a systematic evaluation plan while another evaluates impulsively. Institutional politics, funding sources, staffing, demographics of the student population, type of institution, type of program, and time are some elements that influence the status of evaluation in a particular program.

In a survey of 181 postsecondary two-year and four-year public and private institutions in the United States that had learning assistance programs, 77.3 percent ranked the need to improve the total program as the most important reason for evaluation (Clymer, 1978). "To give staff performance feedback" received the second highest ranking, "to retain and/or increase funding" was ranked third, and to determine accreditation was the least important reason for evaluation.

Compare those reasons for evaluation with the purposes identified by the authors of this issue. Clowes suggests that a theoretical purpose of evaluation is to ask an appropriate question as well as answer it. Majer and Myers propose that the general purpose of evaluation is to provide information in order to make decisions to answer questions about program

C. C. Walvekar (Ed.), *New Directions for College Learning Assistance: Assessment of Learning Assistance Services*, no. 5. San Francisco: Jossey-Bass, 1981.

improvement and effectiveness. Moore and Boylan present a potpourri of purposes for evaluation, while Smith, Brown, and I focus on more specific purposes such as staff performance and student performance.

The major purpose of evaluation is decision making. Through evaluation, we make decisions about program components: learners, staff, budgets, instruction, materials, learning environment, systems and procedures, and goals. Evaluation provides the information that we need to make decisions about these components. Specifically, through analyzing collected data, decisions are made to install, modify, revise, or delete program components or parts of the components with the hope that improvements will result. This is a simple description of evaluation. In practice, it is not so simple because we must also make decisions about what to evaluate, when to evaluate, how to do it, how to use the results, to whom to show the results, and how to institute new programs or implement changes in established programs without disrupting what is already working. Evaluation is a lot of work. In some cases, the effort put forth in evaluation does not yield a better, more efficient, or more effective program or program component. Furthermore, the changes that are made may actually be worse, or less efficient, or less effective than what existed before evaluation. Why bother, then?

We bother because we want to improve. We bother because we want to deliver services that help students learn and succeed. We bother because we want to have some evidence that our program did indeed have a positive influence on students' learning and success. We bother because we want to show administrators and faculty that we are needed on most postsecondary campuses. We bother because we want to have an impact on instruction and the quality of education that students receive in higher education. We bother because we want "to make a difference," as Myers and Majer put it. We bother because we are a profession that tries to solve problems. Evaluation enables us to do all this.

Several authors of this volume have demonstrated the power of evaluation to solve problems. Darrel Clowes begins with the problem of a muddle of different approaches to evaluation and ends with a model of evaluation. Smith and Brown develop the problem-solving capability of performance objectives. The chapter written by Majer and Myer on using research designs elaborates on the problem-solving nature of evaluation as a means to answer questions. Robert Moore identifies the purpose of context evaluation as solving problems. My chapter includes a process for helping students to solve learning problems.

Change is often a result of problem solving. Likewise, change is often a result of evaluation. The message of evaluation as an agent of change moves like a wheel through this volume. Evaluation is the hub, programs components are the spokes, and change is the movement that results. People make the evaluation wheel move, and, of course, the wheel does not always move forward. Not all change is good change. Nevertheless, change frequently is necessary for our programs and students to improve. In practice, then, evaluation can respond to the reality of what needs change and serve as a vehicle to cause change.

Change is scary and, to many, so is evaluation. But we must overcome the fear of change and evaluation because both are realities of our time. Both are inevitable as we observe decreasing funds and increasing student problems. This volume attempted to show how, through evaluation, learning assistance programs can meet these challenges in our changing educational environment.

References

Clymer, C. "An Analysis of Evaluation Practices of Learning Assistance Programs in Selected Institutions of the United States." Unpublished doctoral dissertation, Department of Curriculum and Instruction, New Mexico State University, 1978.

Annotated Bibliography

Astin, A. W. *Four Critical Years: Effects of College on Beliefs, Attitudes, and Knowledge.* San Francisco: Jossey-Bass, 1977.

This work reports the results of a ten-year longitudinal study on student development conducted by the Cooperative Institutional Research Program of the American Council on Education. It provides detailed information on the impact of college attendance on student values, attitudes, self-concept, achievement, and career development.

Cross, K. P. *Accent on Learning: Improving Instruction and Reshaping the Curriculum.* San Francisco: Jossey-Bass, 1976.

Cross reviews the literature on efforts to provide alternative instruction to the "new college student." Following a summary of these efforts, the author proposes some of her own alternatives for improving the quality of postsecondary instruction.

Dressel, P. L. *Handbook of Academic Evaluation: Assessing Institutional Effectiveness, Student Progress, and Professional Performance for Decision Making in Higher Education.* San Francisco: Jossey-Bass, 1976.

A major benefit of this book is its emphasis on evaluating student service agencies, and thus, affective influences in higher education. This book also emphasizes the relationship of political issues to evaluation. The section on evaluating the learning environment is especially helpful.

C. C. Walvekar (Ed.). *New Directions for College Learning Assistance: Assessment of Learning Assistance Services*, no. 5. San Francisco: Jossey-Bass, 1981.

Guba, E. G., and Lincoln, Y. S. *Effective Evaluation: Improving the Use-fulness of Evaluation Results Through Responsive and Naturalistic Approaches.* San Francisco: Jossey-Bass, 1981.

This is an argument for the use of naturalistic inquiry methods where they are appropriate. The review of evaluation as a field is exceptional and prepares the base for supporting responsive evaluation as the approach of choice. The arguments are lucid and often elegant, the distinctions helpful, and the writing clear. Here one finds excellent minds engaged in a fascinating and yet practical probing of the purpose, limits, and proprieties of evaluation.

McConkey, D. D. *MBO For Nonprofit Organizations.* New York: American Management Associations, 1975.

This book provides managers in nonprofit organizations with a practical introduction to the management by objectives system, including its components, operations, and applications. Examples from specific nonprofit organizations using MBO illustrate the benefits of this system.

Newman, J. E., and Hinrichs, J. R. *Performance Evaluation for Professional Personnel.* Scarsdale, N.Y.: Work in America Institute, 1980.

Reviewing current literature, the author defines and describes the purposes of performance evaluation, addresses the issue of evaluating professionals, describes facets of performance evaluation, and discusses the feedback process. The second half of the book contains abstracts of articles written on performance evaluation.

Patton, M. Q. *Qualitative Evaluation Methods.* Beverly Hills, Calif.: Sage, 1980.

Patton provides an excellent guide to both when and how to use qualitative methods. The sections on evaluation design and on the nature of qualitative data are especially helpful. This book then carries through the implementation stage with sections on collecting and analyzing qualitative data. A real strength is the light writing style and brilliant use of parables as chapter beginnings.

Popham, J. W. *Educational Evaluation.* Englewood Cliffs, N.J.: Prentice-Hall, 1975.

This book traces the historical development of educational evaluation and describes major evaluation concepts and terms. The author categorizes evaluation designs using a very understandable system. Chapters on criterion-referenced measurement and affective measurement are quite helpful. Popham's easy style of writing makes this book a delight to read.

Roueche, J. E., and Snow, J. J. *Overcoming Learning Problems: A Guide to Developmental Education in College.* San Francisco: Jossey-Bass, 1977.

The results of a national survey of developmental education programs are presented along with detailed descriptions of twelve "exemplary" programs designed to assist the underprepared college learner. On the basis of survey results, the authors suggest models for the delivery of services to underprepared college learners.

Smith, H. P., and Brouwer, P. J. *Performance Appraisal and Human Development.* Reading, Mass.: Addison-Wesley, 1977.

Focusing on utilizing human talent effectively, this book discusses the psychological aspects of performance appraisal. It provides information on the principles of human growth and development and how these principles relate to performance appraisal. Sample performance appraisal interviews are included to demonstrate effective techniques for managers.

Sullivan, L. L. *Sullivan's Guide to Learning Centers in Higher Education.* Portsmouth, N.H.: Entelek, 1979.

This is a report of a survey of learning assistance centers in postsecondary institutions in America and Canada. Its strengths are a good response rate (about 50 percent) and volumes of data arranged in every conceivable way. This study updates Devirian's 1974 study and provides baseline data. Its weaknesses are a lack of definition of learning assistance centers, which clouds the findings; poor descriptions of the methodology, so independent interpretations are impossible; and lack of extensive interpretation of the data.

Index